FOOTBALL'S QUICK PASSING GAME

VOLUME 2:

MORE ADVANCED ROUTES

Andrew Coverdale
Dan Robinson

COACHES CHOICE

ISBN: 1-57167-156-0
Library of Congress Catalog Card Number: 97-69611

Book Design: Michelle A. Summers
Cover Design: Deborah M. Bellaire
Cover Photos: Photo Courtesy of 49ers Report
Develomental Editor: Joanna Wright

Coaches Choice Books is a division of: Sagamore Publishing, Inc.
                                           P.O. Box 647
                                           Champaign, IL 61824-0647
                                           Web Site: http//www.sagamorepub.com

DEDICATION

This book is dedicated to A.J. Rickard, who several years ago gave an impetuous young coach his first opportunity in the profession, and who is among the finest coaches I have ever known in any sport, at any level. My deepest thanks for everything you've done.

—A.C.

This book is dedicated to Coach Ken Kaufman, my mentor, my friend, a first-class gentleman, and one of the finest judges of young football talent in the game of football. Although Coach Kaufman is retired, he taught me most of what I know about coaching young people. I shall always cherish the years he spent on my staff at Northwestern High School.

—D.R.

CONTENTS

"The quick passing game? Oh yeah, you mean like the Slant and the Hitch and the Fade. Sure we've got that. Everybody's got that. What else is there to it?" This type of reaction is probably not uncommon among coaches in America, and logically leads to the question, "why write a whole book on something everybody already does?" The reasons are numerous. First, the simple fact is that, to our knowledge, no such authoritative, comprehensive book exists that details this mode of attack. Secondly, the number of ways to attack with the quick passing game have grown vastly over the past several years, and many of these new ideas are on the very cutting edge of how offenses are dealing with defenses' evolution. Third, and perhaps most importantly, the quick passing game, as a quotation like the one above would indicate, is, in our opinion, a widely underutilized, "taken for granted" way of moving the football that has vast potential to move the chains, increase offensive efficiency on a play-to-play basis, and create numerous opportunities for the best athletes on the field to do what they do best in the open field. Having a full understanding of what it can do within an offense and how to best teach and implement it can be a real plus for any team, for reasons that will be thoroughly spelled out throughout the text. Some coaches will find use for this book as a reference tool; some will find an entire, untapped resource that they can use to make substantial improvements in their scheme.

We would, of course, be remiss in writing any book if we did not acknowledge all the men who have gone before us in advancing offensive football in general, and the quick passing game in particular. As with our previous work, we owe large debts to coaches such as Sid Gillman, Don Coryell, Bill Walsh, and a whole host of contemporary colleagues for their innovations in this area of football. Ideas incorporated into this work have come from a diverse array of sources, ranging from Hanover College to the Green Bay Packers to Wayne State University. A large percentage of the material in this book is not original, and so its strength lies not in being revolutionary, but in the quality of those sources from whom it is drawn and the comprehensiveness and detail with which it breaks down concepts into teachable, useful blocks that can result in very tangible benefits for the reader. It is our sincere hope as fellow coaches that you reap a whole host of those benefits from the pages that follow.

Andrew Coverdale
Dan Robinson

B	General symbol for any type of linebacker
C	Cornerback
D	"Dime" player—6th defensive back substituted for a LB
	Also a general symbol refering to defenders in a controlled drill
E	Defensive End
F	Free safety
J	"Joker"—combination rush/drop player in a nickel defense
M	Middle linebacker, either "Mike" or "Mac"
N	Nose tackle, or "Nickel" player—substituted 5th defensive back
R	Symbol for a receiver in a controlled drill situation
S	"Sam," or strongside outside linebacker
SS	Strong safety
T	Defensive tackle
V	General symbol refering to any defensive player
W	"Will," or weakside outside linebacker

Ⓥ   Circle indicates a defender who is the quarterback's primary read or whose movement is key to our thought process in the play design

[V]   Box indicates either a "danger player" to the read or some sort of secondary or pre-snap key for the quarterback.

─────o   Indicates a defender's *pre-snap* movements/adjustments

─────   Indicates a defender's *post-snap* movements/adjustments

— — —   Shows possible *alternate post-snap* movements and how an offensive player would adjust to such movement.

· · · · ·   Indicates the path of a thrown pass.

- - - - -   Shows a defender matched up in man-to-man coverage with the receiver to whom the line connects him.

●────×   Shows an offensive player going in motion prior to the snap; "x" marks the point where he should be at the snap of the ball.

⊘   Shows original position of an offensive player who has shifted.

↑ ↓   Indicates one person stepping *on* to the line of scrimmage as another steps *off*, possibly as a precursor to pre-snap motion.

CHAPTER 1

The "Quick Smash" Route

The "Quick Smash" is one of the quick passing game's most important evolutions against the hard corner styles of defense that have been used to shut down its high-percentage throws on the outside. We were originally introduced to this package in watching film of Wayne State University, and were attracted instantly to its ability to quickly strike against two deep secondaries. Since then, we've found other good uses and variations related to it.

This route package is designed to isolate a cornerback on the edge of the field and quickly get a receiver behind him and a receiver in front of him in such a relationship that he cannot cover both. The quick timing with which it attacks the defense is the key to this route. This timing is one of the things that gives the Quick Smash a number of very positive dimensions. Some of the most important of these dimensions include the following:

1. *Its outstanding ability to attack traditional Cover 2 with low corners.* A properly run Quick Smash with the right type of throw can get to the hole behind a low corner very rapidly for a large chunk of yardage.

2. *The ability to attack "reading" Cover 2 cornerbacks who try to cause problems for the read by "slow playing."* The quarterback has a very simple read that is executed very quickly off a three-step drop and is designed to get the ball driven into someone *before* the cornerback can play his games.

    For that reason, the three-step Quick Smash can be used as an alternative to the more traditional five-step Smash. The speed of its execution allows hash safeties less time to be a factor in the play, and the read is more immediate and direct, which results in less of a "cat-and-mouse" game with the cornerback.

    This simple read on a fast tempo also minimizes the effects of disguised coverage, since we are merely working off the reaction of a single man. Many times, teams show the same Cover 2 shell time after time and try to confuse offenses by rolling from that to Quarters, Inverts, Cover 4, and the like. All of that activity has no effect on our basic, quick read.

3. *It is an excellent play to call or check to against the blitz.* As has already been noted, the Quick Smash can be delivered quickly; it can also be protected with eight men, and takes advantage of the inside leverage man coverage that often accompanies blitzes. A good athlete is given a tremendous amount of room to the outside to which he can run on this play.

4. *The route has benefits to both the wide and short side of the field.* Depending on the coverage, the Quick Smash can work well to either the wide or short side of the field. Each version has a slightly different personality, creating different problems for defenses.

5. *Quick Smash is a pass that can serve as either a high-percentage "chain mover" or as a downfield strike.* Depending on down and distance, formation, and coverage, this package gives us the ability to emphasize a 6-yard Hitch , or a Quick Smash that can rip off chunks of 18 to 25 yards at a time.

6. *It has the built-in capability to deal with most any coverage.* Taught and executed correctly, the combination of the Hitch and the Quick Smash cuts usually gets at least one person open against most basic coverages. Against Cover 1, Cover 2, Cover 3, Cover 4, or Quarters, someone within the simple read should come free; therefore, the Quick Smash is a play that the quarterback will rarely need to check out of. Generally, some sort of special technique within those coverages is required to stop the pass.

7. *Quick Smash is an excellent route in the Red Zone.* A great deal of an offense's success has to do with how successful they are at scoring once in the red zone, or from the opponent's 25 yard line in. The Quick Smash is an excellent way to attack in this area because of many of the qualities already mentioned that are at a premium in the Red Zone: the ability to create separation from man defenders, the capacity to make use of all kinds of field space, and the ability to throw very quickly and be fully protected.

High Investment, High Reward
Each of these advantages is great, but it is vital to understand that seeing them occur takes a tremendous amount of practice. Quick Smash is a high investment, high reward pass.

Specifically, a great deal of repetition is required for receivers running the Quick Smash to get the feel of the proper breaking points and angles. The quarterbacks need a lot of work to consistently get the ball to the right spot with the right touch.

The specific techniques of these things are discussed later, but it is important to note that we will always practice this route with someone serving as a safety and a cornerback; it is never practiced strictly "on air." Having people in these positions is important because the finer points like angles, spots, touch, and timing, can only be mastered if practiced with reference points to work against.

Basic 96-196 Quick Smash Route Rules

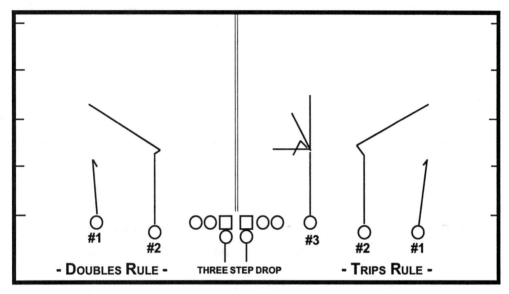

DIAGRAM 1-1
96-196 "QUICK SMASH" PACKAGE

#1: Hitch RUN IT. The receiver runs a six yard Hitch, regardless of the corner's alignment, and should expect the ball. *Exception:* If no one is inside him running a Quick Smash over the top, he should run a normal Hitch/Fade read. He should spin fast, and go north and south for run after catch yardage. Versus a tight cornerback in Cover 2, the receiver should engage/collision him to help the Quick Smash get open above him.

#2: Quick Smash. The receiver's goal is to get into a hole halfway between the corner and safety. He should push to no more than 5-6 yards, nod to lose under coverage, and get there. Several keys help the receiver do his job: Outside release is a must and he should use misdirection steps to ensure it versus a low defender; he should get plenty of split to help himself and line up on the ball; and he should make sure he gets enough distance over the top of the Hitch.

#3: Get Open. The receiver has the freedom to "get open" anywhere above or inside his original position at a depth of seven yards or beyond. He should push vertical for six to seven yards, being certain not to get pushed outside into the Seam's "sandbox." He breaks at 7 based on coverage. His basic guidelines in "getting open" are as follows: if he can stay open by running vertically in his tube, he should do so; if no free safety is in the middle of the field, he should get deep to that area; and he is working against zone coverage with deep help over the top of him, he sits in a hole and makes himself available to the quarterback by getting into his vision.

Quarterback: The quarterback should use a three-step drop and key the cornerback. If he's retreating, giving any ground at all as he hits your third step, he drives it into the Hitch on the number away from the cornerback's leverage. The quarterback should never try to throw the Quick Smash over the head of a cornerback who is giving ground.

If the cornerback is coming up, the quarterback should snap the ball over the top to the Quick Smash, taking him to the sideline to a spot halfway between the cornerback and safety. The Quick Smash must be thrown on rhythm and without hesitation. The quarterback should trust his read.

With few exceptions, this basic read will hold up against any coverage. Against "Cover 3," the corner is still the read. He will probably be retreating, but now a "danger" player exists. The danger player in this special case is the flat player, since he is not being controlled by the Seam as we do in 91/191 Hitch. Therefore, versus Cover 3 the quarterback can either check to 91/191 if he recognizes it pre-snap, or anticipate throwing the Hitch while seeing the flat, or "danger" player, in his peripheral vision.

Throwing the Quick Smash Wide Side vs. Short Side

As noted earlier, the Quick Smash takes on a bit of a different personality and requires a different type of throw when thrown from the hash, or short side, rather than the wide field. In what cases would we like to throw one as opposed to the other? We generally make this determination based on coverage.

Many times, we prefer to throw the Quick Smash against coverages in the Cover 2 family into the boundary. Why? Often, a Cover 2 safety to the boundary side will align no wider or not much wider than the hash mark on his side. This alignment can help give our #2 receiver the vital outside leverage he must gain to be successful. The cornerback also has the Hitch in closer proximity to him, which will tend to bring him down more quickly and help open the hole for the Quick Smash.

The quarterback should know that a boundary throw will be firmer with less loft than one thrown to the wide side; he has a shorter distance to his target. Again, this fact works in favor of the route because it gives the defenders less reaction time.

The coverages against which a wide side Quick Smash are generally preferable are mostly man coverages that do not have a hash safety over the top. In these instances, we like the wide field throw because it forces the man defender to chase our inside receiver through much more space. This open space allows our receiver to accelerate away from his defender, who usually starts with inside leverage, and gives him a lot of area in which to adjust to the ball.

The quarterback will now throw a more lofted ball, taking the receiver into that open space and away from the defender. This lofted type of pass gives the receiver a chance to "run under" the football.

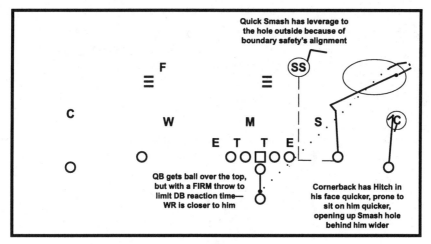

DIAGRAM 1-2
QUICK SMASH INTO THE BOUNDARY VS. COVER 2 SHELL

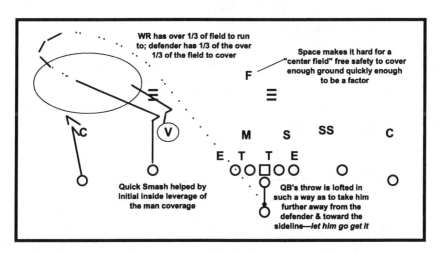

DIAGRAM 1-3
QUICK SMASH TO THE WIDE SIDE VS. MAN COVERAGE

Attacking Coverages with the Quick Smash

Cover 1

When employing the Quick Smash against Cover 1, we generally determine which part of the route we will emphasize based on how tightly or loosely the man coverage is played. Against tight man coverage, we always feel that the Quick Smash by #2 has a great chance to be a big yard-gainer for us. In general, man coverage has a difficult time dealing with the space to the outside that the Quick Smash has to run to, and with good technique, separation can be gained from this low, or "tight" man defender. Good mismatches can be created through different formations and motion once we understand how a defense matches up and deals with pre-snap movement. Some of the specific technique of beating tight man coverage, as well as examples of this formation and motion use, are illustrated below.

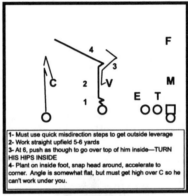

1- Must use quick misdirection steps to get outside leverage
2- Work straight upfield 5-6 yards
3- At 6, push as though to go over top of him inside—TURN HIS HIPS INSIDE
4- Plant on inside foot, snap head around, accelerate to corner. Angle is somewhat flat, but must get high over C so he can't work under you.

DIAGRAM 1-4
QUICK SMASH TECHNIQUE VS.
TIGHT MAN COVERAGE

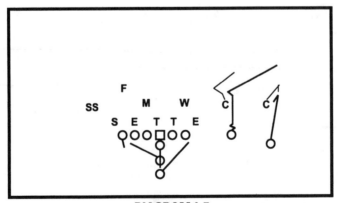

DIAGRAM 1-5
RAY 96 QUICK SMASH VS. TIGHT COVER 1 BLITZ
#2 using good technique to beat low, inside leverage C to the corner, running away from him to the outside.

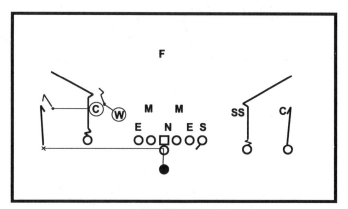

DIAGRAM 1-6
RIP 8 F11 Y196 QUICK SMASH VS. BUMPED, TIGHT COVER 1
Creating a terrible mismatch for W on X out in space

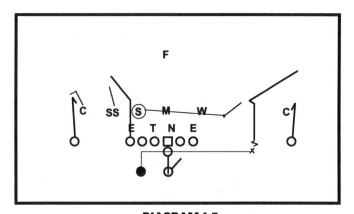

DIAGRAM 1-7
BLACK RIP H8 96 QUICK SMASH VS. LOCKED, TIGHT COVER 1
Forcing a linebacker into wide coverage vs. the Quick Smash

When man coverage is played "softer," or with a "loose" technique, we are more apt to use 96 and 196 as ball control passes to complete the Hitch. We know that most types of man coverage have no true "flat" defender who could threaten the Hitch from inside out, and the softened defender on the outside is giving us the space to throw the Hitch in front of him. However, we do not rule out the Quick Smash portion of the route because it can still be very feasible, especially when mismatches exist with the #2 receivers. Our concerns with it lie in the fact that the defender has a better chance to break down over the top of the route at times (unless a superior job has been done by the receiver of turning his hips), and that if the corner is too soft, he may still be backpedaling into the Quick Smash area when we would need to throw even though he is covering the Hitch man. Again, we come back to our basic read: always throw the Hitch if the cornerback is giving ground.

As in any man coverage, matchups are still very important to us in using this route. In the case of loose man, we will try to do one of two things with our matchups: a) force a player out to cover the Hitch who doesn't normally play wide and thus may be more likely to miss the tackle once the catch is made, or b) create a blatant mismatch for the Quick Smash, knowing that we still have a pretty good guarantee in the Hitch if the deep shot doesn't materialize.

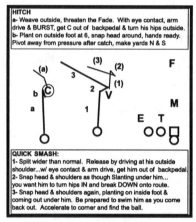

DIAGRAM 1-8
QUICK SMASH TECHNIQUE VS. LOOSE MAN
COVERAGE

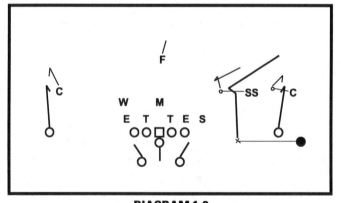

DIAGRAM 1-9
SPLIT ROY X8 96 QUICK SMASH VS. LOOSE COVER 1
Using outside-in motion to influence SS inside and turn his hips; undisciplined bump adjustment by C may also help the leverage of the Hitch

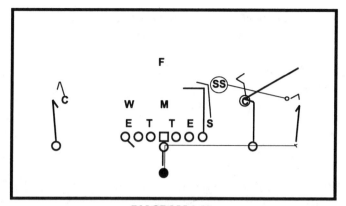

DIAGRAM 1-10
RAM H10 F96 VS. LOOSE COVER 1 W/ SS MOTION ADJUSTMENT
**SS becomes the read player, may not be as good an open-field
tackler vs. the Hitch**

Cover 2 and "Quarters"

Volume 1 Chapter 8 dealt with two distinct ways that Cover 2 is currently being played at many levels: "traditionally," with corners that jam and squat, generally staying level at a depth of 5-6 yards; or with a "pattern read" emphasis, which results in corners running to the deep outside quarter until they are threatened in the flat area. In one sense, this variation makes no difference to us, since the quarterback will be zeroed in on and reading that corner all the way. However, the two variations present different pictures to our players, and we want to ensure that any picture presented to them in a game is something that they have seen numerous times before in practice.

Those "pictures" are depicted below: Diagram 1-11 shows the Quick Smash against a traditional Cover 2, and Diagram 1-12 depicts its use against a pattern-read style of Cover 2.

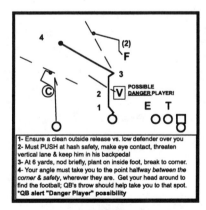

DIAGRAM 1-11
**QUICK SMASH TECHNIQUE VS.
"TRADITIONAL" COVER 2**

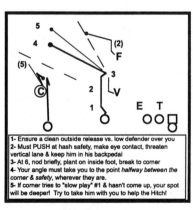

DIAGRAM 1-12
**QUICK SMASH TECHNIQUE VS.
"PATTERN READING" COVER 2**

The two "pictures" have only two major differences. First, the low defender over #2 in traditional coverage may get fast width and depth and become a "danger" player (see chapter on quarterback technique), while in the pattern-read version he "walls" #2 off as long as that receiver works vertical. Second, because of the pattern read technique, the cornerback could end up deeper in the latter example, forcing the Quick Smash to take a steeper angle to get to his "halfway between" point.

Since the same read stays intact, almost any distribution of the route we put together should have an excellent chance against any type of Cover 2. One of the most basic yet effective things that can be done is to provide the quarterback with two identical sides with mirrored Quick Smash combinations and allow him to choose the side he likes best. Our "Flex" set provides this option.

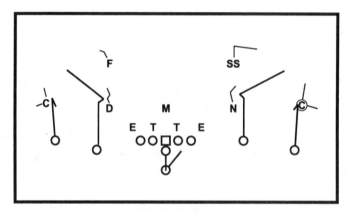

DIAGRAM 1-13
FLEX 96 VS. COVER 2
QB can choose from two symmetrical sides, reads C

Within the 96 package, we can also take advantage of teams that do not check out of Cover 2 against trips. One method is to use a "Rex Out" set in which the #2 and #3 receivers align a yard apart from each other. Their pairing, as well as the vertical release of #3, should help hold the hash safety on that side, enhancing the open hole for the Quick Smash. If the safety insists on crossing their faces and playing for width, the "Get Open " will naturally slide open in the vertical seam just inside him.

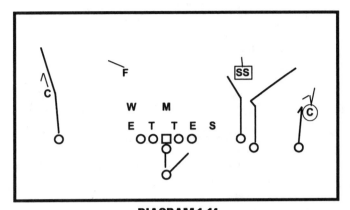

DIAGRAM 1-14
REX OUT 96 QUICK SMASH VS. COVER 2
Vertical release by #3 holds SS vs. teams that stay in Cover
2 vs. Trips

"Squeeze" sets can also have an effective use in attacking Cover 2, particularly if the corners squat. In fact, the more contact they want to make with #1 in this situation, the better.

Essentially, "squeezing" a 96 or 196 Quick Smash drastically changes the coverage angles of both the hash safety and the cornerback. This situation is one of the rare instances in which we prefer throwing a Quick Smash against Cover 2 to the wide field, because the cornerback is being held low and inside while the safety is given a tremendous amount of room to cover outside and over the top. Many times, the Quick Smash will actually end up a number of yards outside and behind the cornerback. Because of the angles and space involved, a hash safety who takes more than one or two backpedal read steps will find himself unable to defend the spot that is being thrown to in time.

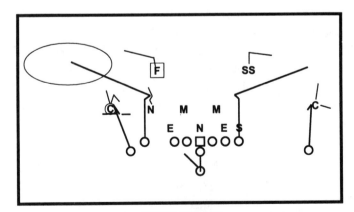

DIAGRAM 1-15
SQUEEZE RIP 9 196 QUICK SMASH VS. COVER 2
Using "Squeezed" Hitch to change angles for corner and safety

Related to the "Squeeze" adjustment for the Quick Smash is its utilization from a "Wing" type set. Again, we are pulling the cornerback down and in and changing the safety's angle to play the Quick Smash.

For the Hitch route used in this pass from a squeezed or wing set, we give him a special adjustment to maximize his effectiveness. The receiver is given a miniature "option" route off his initial break. The depth of his cut is shortened to five yards, and he has the freedom after planting to slide into any hole he feels away from the pressure of short defenders inside and/or outside of him. Two examples of how that technique might work are illustrated below.

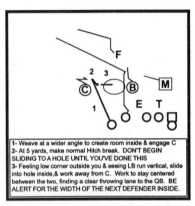

DIAGRAM 1-16
SQUEEZE / WING HITCH ADJUSTMENT:
C stays low, LB walls and works vertical

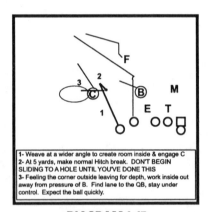

DIAGRAM 1-17
SQUEEZE / WING HITCH ADJUSTMENT:
C runs under Qk Smash, LB works for width

One situation that lends itself well to the Quick Smash from a wing set is "Quarters" coverage, which is essentially played like Cover 2 to one side and Cover 4 to the other. By setting a tight end and wing away from two split receivers, we provide the quarterback two legitimate sides that he can work. The wing side has a chance to get the deep shot to the wide field against the hard corner; the wide side has an excellent shot to get the Hitch open against a soft corner.

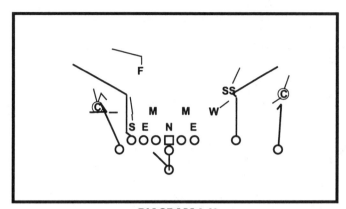

DIAGRAM 1-18
RAY OUT 96 OR 196 VS. QUARTERS COVERAGE
Two workable sides for QB: one to a wing side, one to a spread side.

Cover 3

The Quick Smash is a very viable play against Cover 3 as long as the flat coverage does not widen very quickly in a position to get underneath the Hitch. Cover 3 with wide flat coverage becomes a problem since no one is in place to "control" him inside. If he widens to take away the Hitch, and the cornerback does his job by staying deep and taking away the Quick Smash, we have no play. If the flat coverage doesn't work for fast width, the play is still fine; the Hitch should be open.

Generally, we use one of three approaches to this situation:

1. Create a "check with me" situation where we tell the quarterback that he will get us into 91 Hitch or 96 Quick Smash based on coverage. If he sees Cover 3 pre-snap, he goes to 91 since we can control the flat coverage with the Seam read (see Volume 1 Chapter 6). This approach works as long as we can get a reliable pre-snap read on coverage.

2. Call the 96 Quick Smash and coach the #2 receiver to convert his route to a Seam vs. Cover 3. This technique answers the problem of not always knowing the coverage pre-snap, but takes a lot of practice time. The differences between Cover 1 with a free safety and Cover 3, for example, are not always readily obvious to the quarterback and the receiver on the move.

3. Call 96 Quick Smash without the conversion and use it from formations that will help us in regard to the flat coverage. These sets fall into two basic categories. The first is wide, 2 x 2 sets that allow the quarterback to pick the side where the flat coverage is the least threat. The second is tightened run sets that force the flat coverage to tighten down in a run support position.

Examples of both of these formation ideas are shown below.

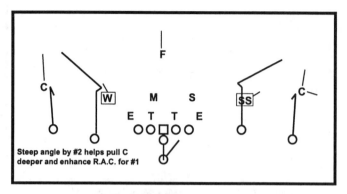

DIAGRAM 1-19
FLEX 96 OR 196 QUICK SMASH VS. COVER 3
Giving QB leeway to choose the side away from most
dangerous flat coverage; should go left here

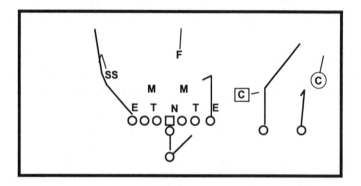

DIAGRAM 1-20
RAM X 96 QUICK SMASH VS. COVER 3
Using a formation with a strong running edge to encourage flat cover-
age into run support alignment and lessen his ability to run under Hitch

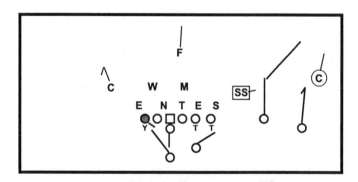

DIAGRAM 1-21
STRONG EAST Y96 QUICK SMASH VS. COVER 3
Unbalanced, run-heavy formation used to pull SS into less
advantageous cover position

The keys to successful plays against Cover 3 are much the same as they are for throwing the 91-191 Hitch against Cover 3: a ball thrown on time to the outside and away from pressure, as well as a tight spin by #1 after the catch that allows him to quickly make yards upfield. If #2 does a good job of deepening his angle and influencing the cornerback, 96 Quick Smash can actually be the preferred way to throw Hitches against Cover 3, because run after catch yards increase when the corner has to attack from a deeper spot.

The quarterback must still intently read the cornerback so that even though he will hit the Hitch 98 times out of 100 against Cover 3, we can still take advantage of an overly aggressive Cover 3 corner by striking deep over his head if he does prematurely jump the Hitch.

Cover 4
The Quick Smash is a very solid concept against Cover 4 and the varying techniques played within Cover 4 for a number of reasons:

1. The outside linebacker over the #2 receiver is often taught to "wall" the #2 receiver as he releases vertical until he sees a break by #1. As hard as he may try, he can not effectively break on the Hitch if proper receiver splits are used.

2. The safety, counting on the short help on #2 from the linebacker, generally jumps into man coverage on him only after the receiver has released vertical for 10 yards. The break of the Quick Smash happens before this spot, so our player has broken and is accelerating to his final spot well before this deep defender has a chance to engage him. If the safety takes any kind of backpedal "read steps" at all, he will never be able to play the Quick Smash at all. As a result, the corner is basically isolated on two men.

3. Cornerback play within this coverage varies from a soft "deep quarter" technique to an essentially man coverage technique. In either case, our basic read will still hold up, either hitting the Hitch in front of a corner, or perhaps throwing to the Quick Smash over the top of him if he plays aggressively on the Hitch.

The picture of all these elements working together is illustrated below.

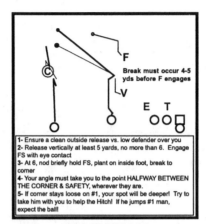

DIAGRAM 1-22
QUICK SMASH TECHNIQUE VS. COVER 4

Illustrated next are two different ways the Quick Smash might be used against Cover 4. The first is a basic split backs, three wide receiver application. In the second, we take advantage of the fact that aggressive cornerbacks sometime anticipate the Hitch from backfield motion and attempt to set up the Quick Smash over his head. It also creates a good matchup for X against an outside linebacker.

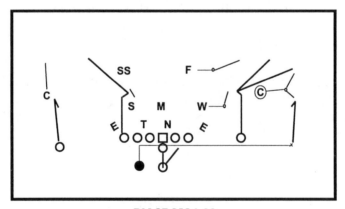

DIAGRAM 1-23
BLACK LIZ H10 96 QUICK SMASH VS. COVER 4
Motion to change DB landmarks, create better matchup
for Quick Smash, and possibly sucker C low

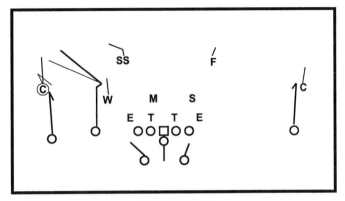

DIAGRAM 1-24
SPLIT LEX 196 QUICK SMASH VS. COVER 4

The "Whip" Tag

The primary tag that we have found almost as much use for as the basic Quick Smash is the "Whip" tag for #1. To us, a "Whip" is a route in which a receiver pushes inside at an angle of approximately 45 degrees as though to cross, trying to turn defenders' hips, and then plants and accelerates straight back to the outside at a depth of 4 to 5 yards.

This tag is very useful against two specific coverages, providing great leverage in different ways against both. The first of these is Cover 4. The "Whip" tag takes advantage of the fact that many Cover 4 cornerbacks immediately work deep to their quarter of the field when #1 releases inside. Combined with the fact that linebacker is running vertical with #2, the Whip will find himself in a lot of open space as he whips back to the outside. The result is a high-percentage four or five-yard throw that has a great chance to make yardage after the catch. Generally, we will use wider sets to attack Cover 4 with the Whip to create more distance between the Whip and outside linebacker. This technique is illustrated below, along with an example of what the whole play might look like.

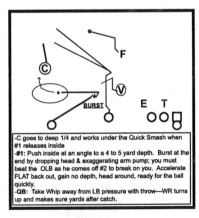

-C goes to deep 1/4 and works under the Quick Smash when #1 releases inside
-#1: Push inside at an angle to a 4 to 5 yard depth. Burst at the end by dropping head & exaggerating arm pump; you must beat the OLB as he comes off #2 to break on you. Accelerate FLAT back out, gain no depth, head around, ready for the ball quickly.
-QB: Take Whip away from LB pressure with throw—WR turns up and makes sure yards after catch.

DIAGRAM 1-25
196 "WHIP" TECHNIQUE VS. COVER 4

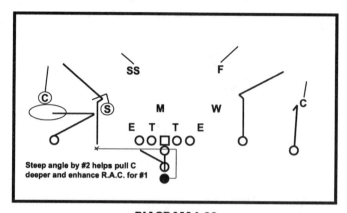

DIAGRAM 1-26
REX H9 196 WHIP VS. COVER 4
Use formation to attack S, who's often slower than W;
wide set creates distance between him and the Whip

Quick Smash routes tagged with a Whip are also outstanding against most forms of man coverage. In this case, the Whip is best when, by formation or motion, #1 ends up two yards or less outside #2. When he releases, he will end up crossing the path of #2, and will cross that path again when he whips back out. The result is that the man covering him is, in the worst case scenario, forced to "bubble" his course, making a break on the Whip route difficult. The better and more likely scenario is that he will make contact with either the #2 receiver or the defender covering the #2 receiver either coming or going. Again, the Whip will be a very short throw, resulting in a great deal of space for the receiver to run to after the catch.

To get #1 in the position we want, a "Squeeze" call is very applicable, as is "Snug" motion to start him wide and motion him in closen pre-snap. The trips rule can also be effective for the Whip against man coverage, creating more traffic for the defender to run through. Illustrations follow.

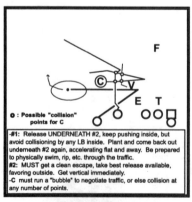

DIAGRAM 1-27
196 "WHIP" TECHNIQUE VS.
MAN COVERAGE

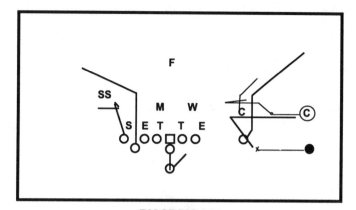

DIAGRAM 1-29
RAY IN X SNUG 96 WHIP VS. COVER 1 FREE
Short motion to a wider #2; basic backside combination
workable also

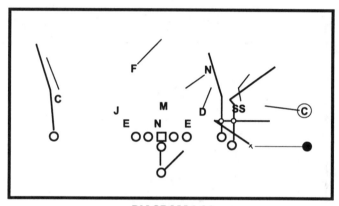

DIAGRAM 1-30
REX OUT Z SNUG 96 WHIP VS. COVER 1 ROBBER
Trips rule to create additional traffic problems

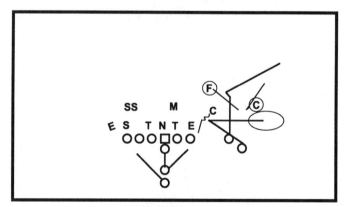

DIAGRAM 1-31
SQUEEZE RAY MAX 96 WHIP VS. BANJOED COVER 1 BLITZ
Static "squeezed" Whip: C switches to #2 on Banjo when #1
crosses, leaving FS out of position to cover #1 when he whips
back out

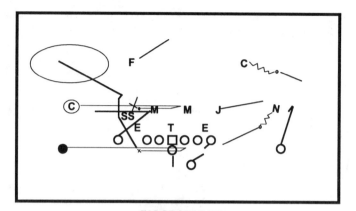

DIAGRAM 1-32
GREEN LARRY 10 X RETURN (COLT) 196 WHIP VS. TIGHT MAN COVERAGE
Focus on the Quick Smash—C forced into a trail position vs. Out by
motion; X releases underneath and outside #1 before release, major
traffic problems getting through to cover Quick Smash. X has a lot of
space to run to because of tightened formation

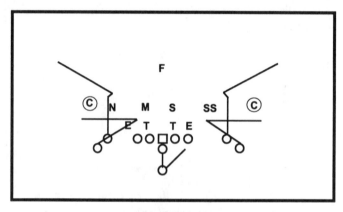

DIAGRAM 1-33
TWIN 96 DOUBLE WHIP VS. COVER 1 FREE
Mirrored Whips give QB ability to go to best matchup or widest field

CHAPTER 2

The "Stop" Route

Introduction and Basic Concept of Attack

The "Stop" route is the natural complement of the Fade because the cosmetics of it and the technique look the same as our Fade/Seam package until the point of the final break of the outside man back downhill to the sideline. It is an outstanding short side route; in fact, we rarely run it to the wide field.

In general, we have found this route to be best against either very good cornerbacks who are smart and quick to react to certain things, or very poor cornerbacks who cannot break on anything. The latter case occurs very rarely at our level; however, in the case of an outstanding defender, he will intuitively recognize the body language of the Fade release, having seen it once or twice, and work to get over the top. He has usually been taught that when the receiver looks back for the ball, he looks back. These reactions create leverage for one of our single receivers to get open breaking back downhill to the outside. An average or mediocre player at corner does not have that reaction, therefore not allowing the same clearance and often obstructing the play through no merit of his own.

The Stop is truly one of the most straightforward ideas we have conceptually in the quick game because there is generally no read on the quarterback's part; we are singling a person or people to run a Stop route on the outside, and we are going to throw the ball there. Most times the quarterback's decision is limited to: a) a pre-snap look to determine which of the two outside Stops (if the formation provides for it) to work based on match-ups, field, or other factors, and b) whether his man is going to be open enough to throw the ball to once the play begins.

In a basic sense, we believe we can run a Stop successfully into most different types of cornerback techniques. Even if he is rolled up tightly, a scenario that might normally chase us out of an out-breaking route, the pattern should work. Why? Even pure "Cover 2" cornerbacks turn their hips to react to the Fade hole briefly if they have no threat to the flat coming from the inside. If they do not, we won't get to this call to begin with because we will keep throwing the Fade part of the sequence over his head.

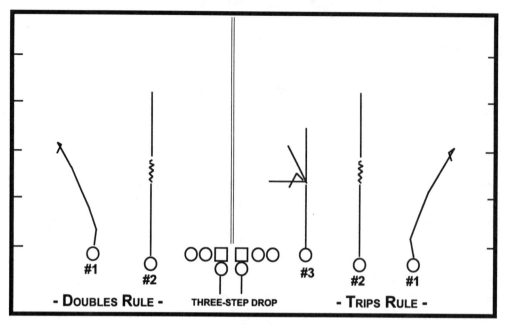

DIAGRAM 2-1
94-194 "STOP" PACKAGE

Basic 94-194 "Stop" Package Rules

#1: Stop. The receiver splits 10-12 yards from the tackle/tight end on his side, creating separation from other underneath coverage while giving himself enough room to operate. From the hash, he splits six to seven yards from the sideline.

The initial release and stem of the receiver route should look exactly like the Fade. Against a soft corner, the receiver jab step inside to turn him initially, gets outside him, and pins him, straightening up and then bursting as if going to the Fade. As he begins this burst, the receiver looks back and lays his hands out as though the ball is coming. Once he sees the defender turn his hips and run upfield, the receiver knows the defender is beaten and begins to bring himself under control, breaking down his hips and driving back downhill to the sideline off his inside foot. In general, the depth of this break will be in the neighborhood of 10 to 12 yards; however, he is breaking when he gets the reaction he wants out of the corner, not at a specific depth.

Against a hard corner, the only thing that changes is that the receiver needs to work very hard to ensure an outside release. From this point, he is pinning, bursting, looking, and breaking in the same manner. If the defender refuses to allow the receiver outside, the receiver should widen him, straighten up briefly at the widest width he will allow and then use an extended burst toward the hole behind him, angling toward a spot about 18 yards deep on the sideline. At this point, one of two things will happen: a) the receiver will get the corner turned and running back toward that hole, in which case he can make his outside break back underneath him to the sideline, or b) the defender will stay short and widened, covering an area, in which case the receiver will have created enough width to plant off his outside foot and snap his head back around to the inside, looking for the ball inside him (see Diagrams 2-3 through 2-5).

#2: Seam. The receiver runs a basic Seam route with a slightly different emphasis. In this case, the route is not a part of a normal read sequence by the quarterback; rather, the receiver is more of a purpose player who needs to ensure the flat coverage does not work underneath the Stop. Therefore, the receiver should work to release outside the flat before straightening him up. Unlike other Seam routes, where being collisioned is disastrous, collisioning is acceptable in this case because the flat defender takes himself out of the play and effectively singles the corner on our Stop route, which is what the offense wants.

If the flat coverage does cross the receiver's face, he should look very quickly, because the quarterback will see the flat defender and get the receiver the ball immediately.

#3: Basic "Get Open" route. The receiver has the freedom to 'get open' anywhere above seven yards over the top of the "box." If no free safety is in the deep middle, the receiver should get deep down the middle as quickly as possible. Against man coverages where there is deep middle help, the receiver will generally cross flat at about seven yards, stabbing outside and either coming underneath him or breaking over the top. It is important that the receiver not wander or get jammed outside his lane into the lane of the Seam.

Quarterback: In a "double width" set, the quarterback should decide which side he will work prior to the snap. What determines this decision will vary, but considerations will include match-ups, field width, and underneath structure. Generally, this pattern is thrown to the short side of the field.

After the snap, the quarterback takes a big three-step drop and bounces up on his shuffle step, focusing on the receiver he has chosen and the lane through which he will have to throw to get it there. He is seeing two things: whether or not the outside receiver gets his man turned and running upfield, and if anyone from underneath invades the throwing lane. If the lane is clean and the cornerback turns and runs deep, the quarterback delivers the ball as he sees the receiver's rear end drop. The ball should be placed "right behind his head," bringing him slightly back downhill to the outside. The quarterback should "offset" him slightly to maintain the separation he gets, but be careful not to offset too much, lest he not be able to get back quickly enough. The ball should be one-third of the way to the receiver by the time his head snaps around after his final break.

The only other option is if the offense has a second split receiver and the flat defender really opens up flat to get underneath the Stop. In this case, the quarterback quickly hits the Seam in the area the defender vacated. If neither of these situations exists, the quarterback should throw the ball away.

Alerts Since there is no true *read* on the Stop, quarterbacks are instead given certain "alerts" versus various coverages that help them with the thought process described above.

Forms of man coverage generally present the least worry, since those coverages rarely provide the type of help that threatens the Stop from inside out. Anyone who could potentially fit this bill (e.g., a Robber or Double team/"vice" player) will be clearly evident before the snap, and the focus then will primarily become the cornerback and whether he turns enough to allow the Stop to be open.

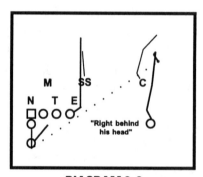

DIAGRAM 2-2
"STOP" VS. MAN COVERAGE
SS runs with Seam; no one to work underneath the Stop

Coverages where the cornerback is rolled up, most notably "Cover 2" and "Cover 3 Cloud," pose the most potential concern, because a defender is aligned in a place before the snap that could cause problems for the throw if he is not moved. This man will demand the quarterback's attention. Receivers against a hard corner should have a real sense of urgency to release outside and threaten the Fade hole to get this movement.

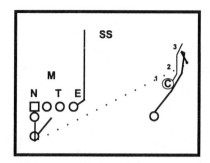

DIAGRAM 2-3
"STOP" VS. HARD OUTSIDE CORNER ex. 1
1) C allows outside release
2) WR gets his width, and then straightens
up to straighten C up and turn his hips
3) WR makes normal Stop break, is led
slightly further back downhill than normal.

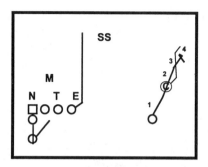

DIAGRAM 2-4
"STOP" VS. HARD OUTSIDE CORNER ex. 2
1) C won't allow outside release
2) WR attacks Fade hole, presses for width
3) C turns hips to run with, so WR can break
back inside underneath him and
4) complete his normal Stop break

Against straight "Cover 3" with a soft cornerback and a strong safety responsible for the flat, we still see the cornerback, but our concern shifts to the strong safety. Why? The corner, by definition, should play deep in such a way that will make it difficult for him to defend the Stop. The strong safety, however, could pose a problem to the throwing lane. If this problem arises, we need the quarterback to see it quickly so he can connect with the Seam as quickly as possible.

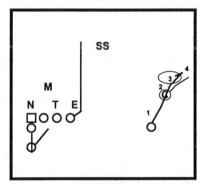

DIAGRAM 2-5
"STOP" VS. HARD OUTSIDE CORNER ex. 3
1) C won't allow outside release
2) WR presses for width, but C keeps widening,
maintains outside leverage
3) WR chases his inside hip to keep widening him
4) Stops in his tracks to inside on normal timing,
open because of width created by C

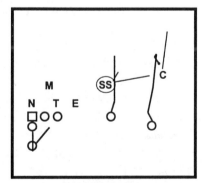

DIAGRAM 2-6
"STOP" VS. COVER 3
Stop works against soft corner;
QB must be aware of SS and
throw Seam if he flies

Favored Sets

Because the structure of the route requires that we create the leverage for it by our call, specific considerations exist for the types of sets we use in constructing Stop calls. While no one set gives us all of the advantages that follow, we try to put as many of them together at once as we can.

1. *Double width sets.* Having a "double" width formation is helpful because it provides the choice of picking the best matchup, not limiting the quarterback to a single Stop route.

2. *Sets used in the running game.* Sets that we also employ heavily in our running game are often preferable, because those short, "edge" defenders who could conceivably work wide underneath the Stop will be more apt to play in tighter, run support positions.

3. *Formations that are easily protected.* Because the Stop requires the quarterback to hold the ball longer than any of our other quicks, protection is a real consideration in the formations we use. Ideally, we like to have at least the potential in our sets to protect with eight, with seven usually being the minimum. We do not necessarily need the extra men in the pattern to open things up, because we are basically working the edge of the field only to a single player. In today's football, being able to match up one-on-one is often no guarantee of being protected, and we will exchange a superfluous route for the ability to double team hard-rushing ends and tackles.

   Often, if we have the choice between protecting with two backs and a tight end or a back and a tight end, we'll choose the latter because we help get bodies on bodies quicker and force rushers to take a wider course.

4. *Two wide people on the same side.* Having two split players on a side is a plus because it provides leverage on the defense's flat defender. With an extra wide player, we can use his release and his Seam route to help control the man that could otherwise take away the Stop.

5. *Trips looks to throw weak.* For the same reasons that the singled Slant route can be an excellent concept away from trips (i.e., the fact that trips sets often force a "slide" of linebackers to the trips side to be sound, opening up weakside throwing lanes), singled Stop routes can be even better. Why? We do not need the short defender on the weakside as tightly compressed to be able to throw through the Stop lane, because the route starts, remains, and is thrown on the outside. Sometimes with the Slant, a linebacker aligned just slightly off the hip of the weakside end can open quickly to the Slant lane with the Slant coming inside, and the offense no longer has a play. A linebacker aligned that way against a Stop would have not have the same opportunity. Weakside flat

defenders must align wide and continue to work for width to have any chance to get in the Stop lane. This maneuver opens up either the weakside running game or the strongside passing game.

6. *Sets equally conducive to the Fade and the Stop.* Against teams who scout and recognize formation tendencies well, we would ideally like to use the same sets to run both the Fade and the Stop. If we find sets that we can use effectively for both, we can use them to run the Fade one game and the Stop the next, or start an individual game running the Fade out of it and going to the Stop later on. This element is a key to having success against the best coaches and defenders on our schedule.

Some examples of sets we will use throughout a season and how they are useful in running the Stop follow.

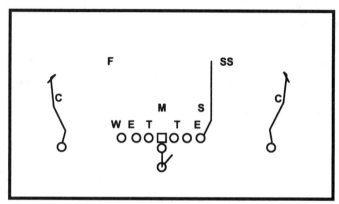

DIAGRAM 2-7
94-194 STOP FROM "RAM"

Our "Ram" set gives us the flexibility of having two wide people on either side to choose from. It is a set from which we run a lot. It generally commands some run support on the edge, and can be used to protect with eight people, providing two tight ends with which to do it. The only possible weakness revolves around the fact that neither side has a second split player, which could make it more difficult to control flat coverage.

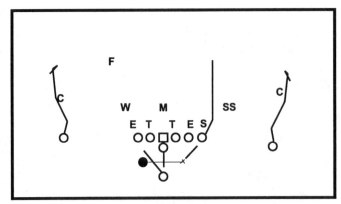

DIAGRAM 2-8
94-194 STOP FROM "WEAK RIP F SHUFFLE"

This formation has many of the same benefits, and in some games may get more of a reaction as a running set. However, it leaves a short, open edge on the weak side for potential speed rushers, and the two backs in protection may not provide the same physical strength that a tight end and a back would. Sequencing Stops with Fades from this is also less likely, unless we are playing a pure man coverage team.

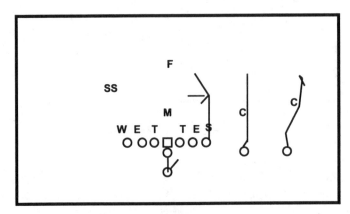

DIAGRAM 2-9
94 STOP FROM "RAM X"

This set is probably one of the two or three best overall sets for the Stop; it is an excellent run and protection set and can be used with Fades as well. The flat coverage is controlled by the second split receiver. This set often dictates some form of Cover 3 when teams check their coverage, so a softer cornerback is gained for our Stop outside. The disadvantages are that we lose the second Stop on the other side, and the set invites rotated and rolled up coverages and unusual backside blitzes that are not to our advantage.

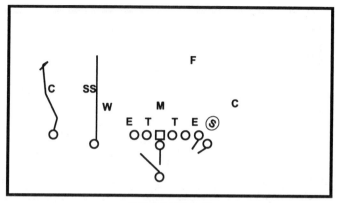

DIAGRAM 2-10
194 STOP FROM "LARRY PLUS"

This formation is both a great running set and a great Fade sequence set, bringing with it the ability to control the strong safety with the slot receiver. It also has the unique benefit of being able to load the protection to handle a specific, dominant outside rusher with a backside tight end-wing double team. The minuses of this set include the lack of a second wide Stop and the one open edge that shortens opponents' rush angles.

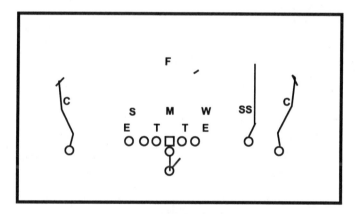

DIAGRAM 2-11
94-194 STOP FROM "LIZ 8"

This formation provides the best overall package in terms of route leverage, having both a second receiver on a side to control underneath coverage *and* a second wide player to give the quarterback a choice. Against certain defensive structures, like the one shown above, it can create a great situation for the single receiver Stop by sinking the flat coverage inside the tight end on that side. It has a shorter edge on one side and can only protect with seven, but sometimes that proves to be more than enough; in those cases "Liz 8" and its mirror, "Rip 9," become two of our top Stop formations of choice.

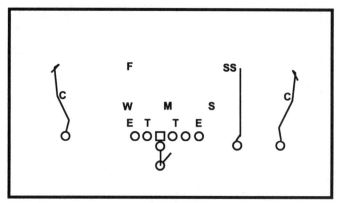

DIAGRAM 2-12
194 STOP FROM "RIP 8"

"Rip 8" is an example of a trips look that puts underneath coverage in a quandary both from the standpoint of supporting the strongside run and defending the strongside pass. This question will often result in some sort of "slide" that opens up the weakside Stop. This formation also gives us the opportunity to protect with seven people by keeping the tight end in.

Movement Concepts

Though we have not yet done a great deal of it, certain types of motion and shifting can be used with the Stop package that definitely enhance the play. Most of them involve a particular type of advantage we're trying to gain on either the cornerback or the underneath structure.

The first type is to simply motion the man to whom we're throwing the Stop across the formation. This motion may prove especially helpful against Cover 2-type teams because having this man on the move at the snap of the ball can help him gain the outside release that is so vital to the route.

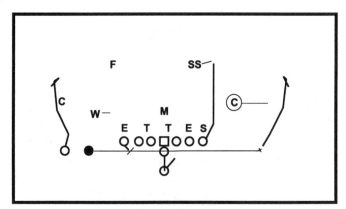

DIAGRAM 2-13
LION X Z10 F94 STOP VS. COVER 2
Putting the corner on the move to help outside release

The next option is to motion the Stop receiver out of the backfield to the widest position on a side. This motion often elicits "vanilla" secondary adjustments, and the man sent to cover this motion man is either a) a linebacker who has been locked into this coverage and is at a physical disadvantage, or b) a secondary player who ends up playing soft because of where he is coming from and the fact that he will be primarily concerned with stopping any sort of deep route. All of these factors work in favor of the Stop. We will often sequence this in reverse order with the Fade, trying to draw a defender down with the Stop the first time, then using the same set and motion to run the Fade by them if their feet halt in anticipation of breaking on the Stop. Two examples of this type of motion are illustrated below.

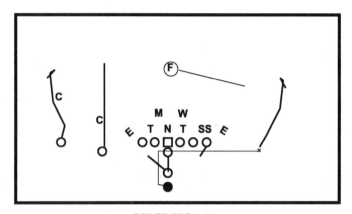

DIAGRAM 2-14
LARRY H10 Y94 VS. COVER 1 WITH FS MOTION ADJUSTMENT
Safety coming from high must be concerned with deep throw first—not in good position to break on the Stop

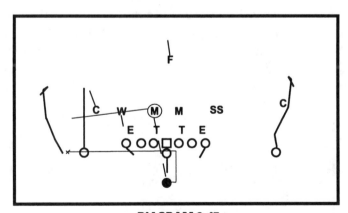

DIAGRAM 2-15
RAM H11 MAX 194 VS. COVER 1 WITH LB LOCKED ON H
Creating a great matchup on a LB in space

The last form of motion we will use with this pattern is outside-in motion by the Seam player. This option is generally used against Cover 3 looks when we are trying to guarantee a release outside the strong safety by the Seam to hinder his progress and ensure that the Stop is singled up.

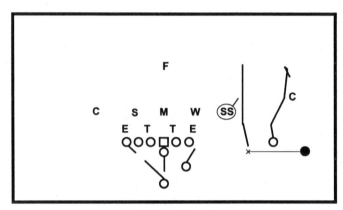

DIAGRAM 2-16
WEAK RAY X8 MAX 94 STOP VS. COVER 3
Using outside-in motion to pin flat coverage

Special shifts can create situations that enable the Stop to be effectively isolated. Especially in the case of a wholesale shift that changes formation strength, a hurried or vanilla defensive adjustment can be created in which the flat defender is out of position. When motion is added to a shift to change strength twice, this problem is even more pronounced.

The simplicity of the Stop really helps us make full use of our shifting and movement packages. At times, such extensive movement can cause confusion for the quarterback as much as it does defenders, but the simple read on the edge of the defense keeps this confusion from being a problem no matter what sort of chaos is occurring on the defensive side of the ball.

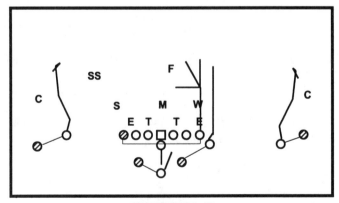

DIAGRAM 2-17
SHIFT TO RIP PLUS 94 STOP

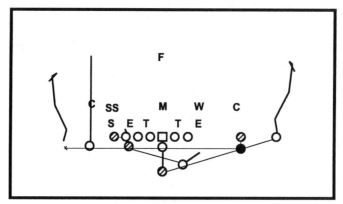

DIAGRAM 2-18
SHIFT TO GREEN LIZ 10 X11 Y94 STOP

CHAPTER 3

The "Turn" Route

In a 1995 *Sports Illustrated* article, an NFL team who employs a version of this route (known in their terminology as "Stick") talked about having thrown it 32 times in their nine games, up to that point. Throwing against the best linebackers and defensive backs anywhere, 27 of the passes had been completed, and two additional ones dropped.

We tell our players that while we may not have NFL talent, we're not playing against it either, and we expect a similar completion percentage. This expectation has not proven unrealistic for us; in fact, if you were to ask our current quarterback to name his favorite passes in our offense, this one would appear in his top three.

The keys to this package are the extreme quickness with which it attacks, the short distance of the throws involved, and the simple two-on-one leverage that is created on an underneath defender.

The basic premise of the "Turn" is to take one receiver quickly to the flat at a depth of one to two yards (i.e., a "Shoot" route) and have a receiver immediately inside him push upfield six yards and turn outside (the "Turn" route). The defender on whom we key, the first short defender inside the corner, must either widen with the quick Shoot, in which case the Turn breaks right into the void he left, or hang in the vicinity of the Turn, which creates an opening for the Shoot. The sheer speed with which all this takes places keeps other defenders from being substantially involved in defending either of the routes; the ball is gone before they can react effectively.

This route has been one of the key elements in the expansion of our quick passing game overall, because it allows us to attack a different portion of defensive structures, and is not in any way dependent on having a soft corner outside.

In terms of how we construct rules and assignments, the Turn is a bit different from the rest of our quick package because it has a distinct frontside and backside and does not operate from a "mirrored" definition. The backside routes are built to get into seams that result from the underneath structure's wholesale slide to the frontside to take away the Shoot and Turn.

As with the other quick routes, the definitions do change on the frontside depending on whether we have two or three receivers there. In a two-receiver distribution, the Shoot and Turn stand on their own, while we add a "Read Go" on the outside of a three-receiver rule. These two forms of the Turn take on distinctly different looks and create different types of opportunities for us.

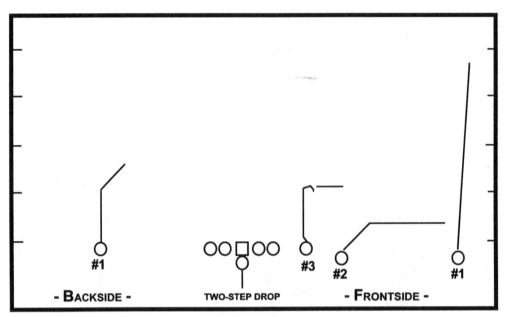

DIAGRAM 3-1
95-195 "TURN" PACKAGE: *"TRIPS," OR 3 RECEIVER RULE*

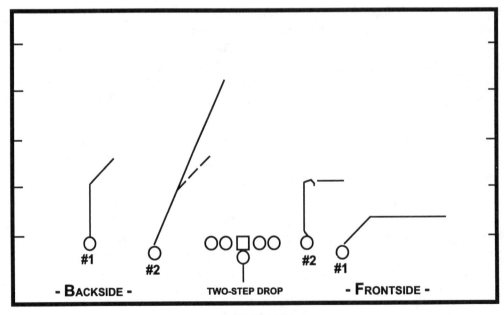

DIAGRAM 3-2
95-195 "TURN" PACKAGE: *"DOUBLES," OR 2 RECEIVER RULE*

95-195 "Turn" Package Rules

Frontside

#1 (3 receiver rule): "Read Go." The receiver takes the maximum split allowable, at least 16 yards from the tackle if we are in the middle of the field, works hard for an outside release against any hard corner and runs a full-speed Go. The only thing that would cause him to adjust this route is if, after releasing, he feels a hard corner let him go and stay short and look back inside. In this case, the receiver needs to throttle his route down in the seam behind the defender, being aware of the hash safety's relationship to him. The receiver should look for the ball and keep adjusting away from the safety.

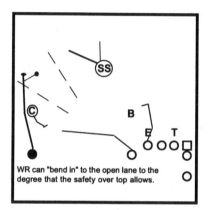

DIAGRAM 3-3
SQUATTED CORNER COLLAPSES ON SHOOT—#1 SETTLES HIS
"GO" IN THE VOID BEHIND HIM, WORKING INTO AN OPEN LANE
WHILE STAYING OUT OF THE SAFETY'S REACH.

#2 (3 receiver rule) or #1 (2 receiver rule): "Shoot." The receiver works one to two steps past the line of scrimmage and quickly snaps his head around to the flat, looking to get the ball and turn upfield immediately. He should be aware of a short corner collapsing inside to tackle him if he is #2 of 3, though in that case, the split of #1 should have given him room to get turned up. The receiver should be aware that he can not continue accelerating laterally after the catch if a short defender is waiting there.

#3 (3 receiver rule) or #2 (2 receiver rule): "Turn." The receiver takes the best possible release, reestablishing a straight course as soon as he can, then plants and snaps his head around to the outside at six yards. If a defender inside him works quickly to attack him laterally, the receiver should collision, lean on, or pin him with his inside shoulder and accelerate away from the defender, continuing to work to the open void outside him. The ball is likely to be on its way as the receiver spins around. After the catch, he spins 180 degrees and begins splitting defenders, going north and south.

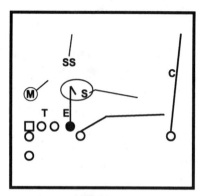

DIAGRAM 3-4
"TURN" ROUTE, 2ND SHORT
DEFENDER DOESN'T APPLY PRES-
SURE FROM THE INSIDE OUT—
Turn is open just by turning around

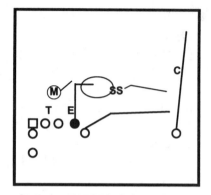

DIAGRAM 3-5
"TURN" ROUTE, 2ND SHORT
DEFENDER APPLIES INSIDE OUT
PRESSURE—
Turn must continue widening into
hole outside

Backside

All backside receivers need to understand their fit within the overall picture of the route. They are given their routes to take advantage of any void left by an extreme defensive overreaction to the frontside. Above all else, they are responsible for being in those voids if they occur.

#1: Slant. The receiver uses basic Slant technique, normal Slant split. He should not be afraid to flatten the route more than normal if he needs separation from the cornerback and the underneath coverage doesn't threaten him while using that angle.

#2: Split. The receiver has a route that could operate on two different levels. His release will take him on an angle through the free safety at 20 to 25 yards deep, looking for the ball in that deep opening if the safety has vacated this area. However, the receiver also needs to look, at an earlier level, for an underneath structure that allows him to be open through the first level of the coverage. In other words, if, as he releases on his angle toward the free safety, he sees that there is no linebacker dropping in such a way to cover him at that level, the receiver should throttle down his route and look for the ball.

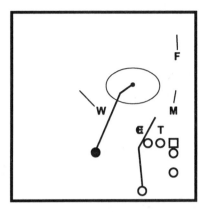

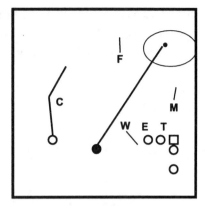

DIAGRAM 3-6
"SPLIT" ROUTE, HOLE OPENS AT
FIRST LEVEL WITH HELP OVER
TOP—Quick look adjustment.

DIAGRAM 3-7
"SPLIT" ROUTE, DEEP MIDDLE
HOLE IS AVAILABLE—
Accelerate to spot 20 yds deep
over center, look for ball, avoid
underneath contact.

Quarterback: The quarterback's basic drop is two steps, and his basic priority is to hit the Turn on an extremely fast rhythm unless he sees that some kind of drop is limiting his access to that throwing lane. If he is throwing the Turn, the ball must be thrown right on the upper part of the receiver's outside number, which will facilitate him catching the ball and spinning outside toward his run after catch more quickly.

A pre-snap identification of where the first short defender inside the cornerback is playing will tell the quarterback who the likely receiver is. If the first short defender inside the corner is a linebacker playing inside the Turn-runner, he likely will work to wall the Turn and not be able to get to the Shoot. If this defender is lined up outside the Turn-player somewhere, he will more likely react to the Shoot and give the offense the Turn.

The quarterback needs to be aware of two special situations. The first is if, in some sort of Cover 2 look, the first short defender takes away the Turn while the cornerback works from the outside-in to squeeze the Shoot. The quarterback should see this problem in his peripheral vision as he turns his shoulders to the Shoot. He should regather his feet, find the outside Go adjusting into the opening behind the corner and hit him.

The other situation is if, through his pre-snap read, the quarterback sees that the underneath coverage has slid over to the route's frontside to the extent that the backside underneath lanes are open. In this case, he will go backside right away.

Using Various Forms of the "Turn"

Three Receiver Packages

Because of the consistent leverage it provides for us, we tend to favor forms of the Turn that give us three receivers to a side. It generally provides us with an open receiver against most any defense we could see, while the 2 receiver rule is more dependent on attacking specific types of coverages.

Our most basic form of a three receiver Turn against Cover 3 is illustrated below.

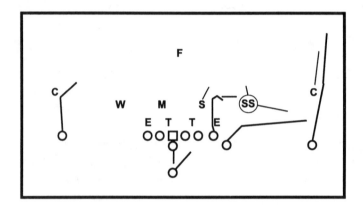

DIAGRAM 3-8
RIP PLUS 95 TURN VS. COVER 3

The next formational element we will introduce to this route is to break #2 and #3 off the formation 3-4 yards to help them operate in a bit more open space. This open space serves two purposes: first, it helps the Turn avoid any sort of jam by defensive ends, and second, it creates more distance between the Turn and the second short defender.

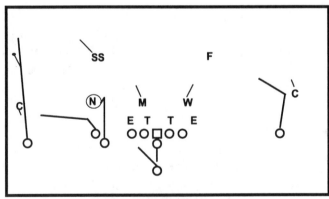

DIAGRAM 3-9
LEX IN 195 TURN VS. COVER 2
Breaking off #2 and #3

As we start having success with this play, the types of sets we employ it from start to become more recognizable to defenses. One of the first things they will do is to slide their linebackers over substantially. In that case we need to look to our backside Slant. Another tactic we can use is to begin to use motion and different formation disguises to cut down on the recognition factor. Both of these dynamics are illustrated in the three examples below.

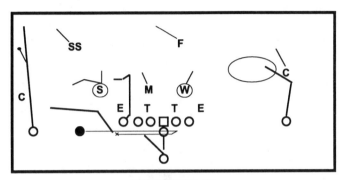

DIAGRAM 3-10
LIZ 9 H RETURN 195 VS. COVER 3 CLOUD
Backside Slant available because of LB slide

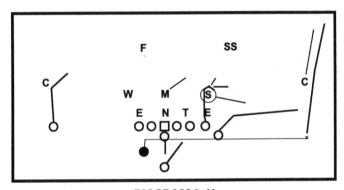

DIAGRAM 3-11
WEAK RIP WING F10 95 TURN VS. COVER 4

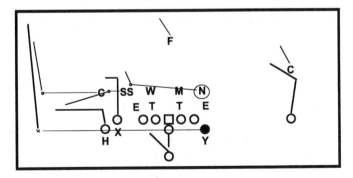

DIAGRAM 3-12
SQUEEZE R 11 Y11 195 TURN VS. BUMPED COVER 1
Create a good matchup vs. a Nickel player forced to play with inside leverage

Adding a "Switch" call changes the jobs of #2 and #3, which opens up some different types of formations that can be used, and also many times serves to build a "wall" for the Shoot that gets him more open. The following split backs distribution is an example.

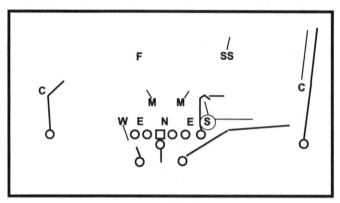

DIAGRAM 3-13
SPLIT RIP 95 SWITCH VS. COVER 4

One of the most potent ways we have of combining some of these elements is to start in a 2 x 2 formation of some sort and motion the remaining back to one side or the other to create a three receiver side. This motion happens very quickly, allowing only a minimal defensive adjustment, and usually keeps the defense from overloading the frontside since they are being pinned by a two receiver backside. Their other option is to make the motion adjustment with the free safety, which opens things up for the backside #2 Split, a potential big play.

It is important to note that we are often forced to use "Hot" 90-190 protection in these cases. Being able to use this protection means repeated, specific drill work with both the quarterback and the line in identifying the hot linebacker and throwing off him. In this case, we are helped by the fact that the quarterback's primary routes serve naturally as "hot" throws.

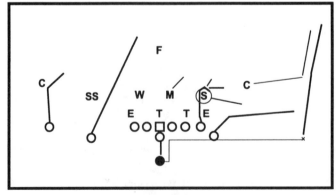

DIAGRAM 3-14
LARRY OUT F10 HOT 95 TURN VS. COVER 3

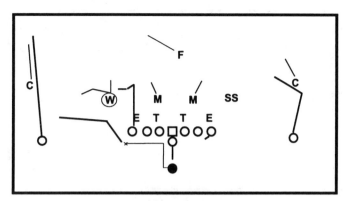

DIAGRAM 3-15
RAM H7 Y195 TURN VS. COVER 3

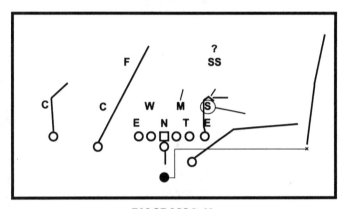

DIAGRAM 3-16
STRONG RAY H10 HOT 95 SWITCH VS. COVER 2 "COWBOY"
Causing problems for "corners over" defenses (see below)

Two Receiver Packages

The 2 x 2 Turn is an ideal way to attack defenses that overload run support and coverage people to "Twins," or a two receiver side away from a tight end. Generally, the two receiver turn is made available to us by a soft cornerback or deep outside defender away from Twins who does not break quickly on short routes, and less than two short defenders on that side. Teams that play "corners over," or "Cowboy" forms of Cover 2 or Cover 3 in which both cornerbacks play over the top of the two receiver side, are ideally suited to be attacked in this way. Diagram 3-16 showed how we might cause problems from such structures using motion and "hot" protection; the next two diagrams illustrate how the 2 x 2 Turn can be used to attack the same types of defense while keeping someone in to block, eliminating the need to go "hot."

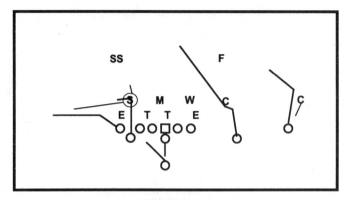

DIAGRAM 3-17
RAY IN 195 TURN VS. COVER 2 COWBOY
Sam linebacker isolated 2 on 1 in a lot of space

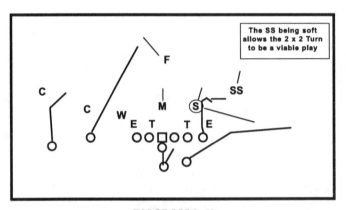

DIAGRAM 3-18
BROWN LARRY 95 SWITCH VS. COVER 3 "COWBOY"

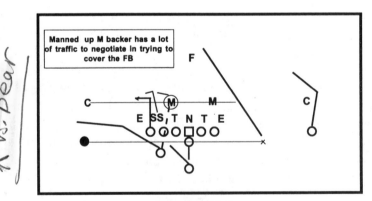

DIAGRAM 3-19
STRONG LIZ Z8 195 SWITCH VS. "LOCKED" COVER 1
Creating good leverage for both the Turn and
the Shoot outside

Motion in various forms by the Shoot receiver is a very good way to create fast movement by the first short defender and open things up for the Turn. Diagrams 3-20 and 3-21 show two different ways to use this motion.

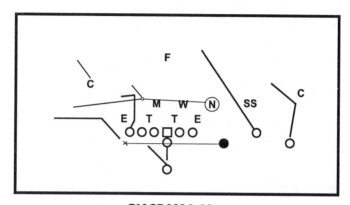

DIAGRAM 3-20
RAY 6 H7 195 TURN VS. NICKEL COVER 3
Defining things clearly by putting the read player on the move

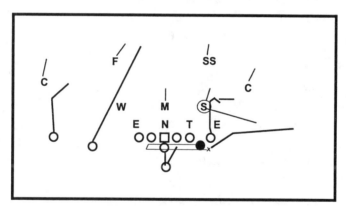

DIAGRAM 3-21
LARRY IN H RETURN 95 SWITCH VS. COVER 4
Quick, stacked release off motion to create definition
problems for pattern-reading OLB

If we play a team that will make backfield motion adjustments with the free safety and we want to create an opportunity to open up the Split but not take the chance of using "hot" protection as in the above versions, the following call would be applicable.

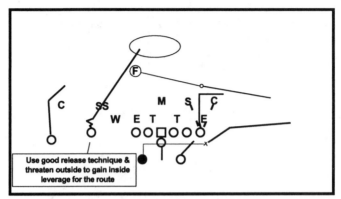

DIAGRAM 3-22
SPLIT LARRY H6 95 TURN VS. COVER 1 WITH FS MOTION ADJUSTMENT
Getting to the "Split" hole down the middle

"Trade" Tag from Bunch

Within our system, we can frequently gain advantages for ourselves by adapting basic routes to "Bunched" formations. In studying some tape of the Detroit Lions, we picked up this version of the "Turn" from a Bunched set that we know as "Trade." Trade simply means that #1 and #2 swap jobs, #1 taking the Shoot and #2 running to #1's normal "Go" landmark from a bunched position. This man clearing from the middle helps to further open things up for the Turn, especially against coverages that try to "wall" or run with vertical releases of #2, such as Cover 4. Two illustrations of this follow, one from a static "Bunch" set, and another in which motion is used. In the latter example, we try to take advantage of the fact that secondaries who see motion to a bunch set anticipate that we are trying to hit a route outside quickly, and good flat defender will work for width in a hurry. That adjustment helps the Turn route, as does the difficulty the quick motion to a nearly "stacked" group of three receivers gives underneath defenders in defining who's who. This confusion makes it more difficult for them to wall people off and break on routes.

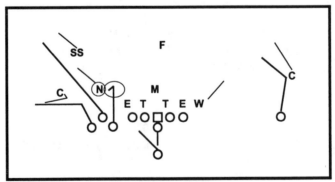

DIAGRAM 3-23
SQUEEZE LEX 7 195 TRADE VS. COVER 3 CLOUD
#2 Go serves as an extra "clear out" player, opens up
space for the Turn when N walls vertical release

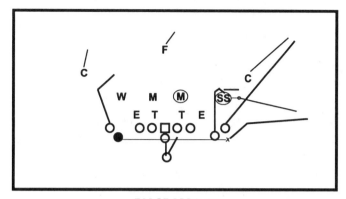

DIAGRAM 3-24
TWIN X10 95 TRADE VS. COVER 3
Motion to widen flat defender quickly in anticipation of
outside break & create a "stacked" grouping

The other benefit brought about by using this "Bunched" version of the Turn is that it can provide a good answer to one of defenses' most common and successful counters to bunch concepts: the jamming of the #2 receiver. Why? Short defenders who want to emphasize the jam on the #2 player must align low, and with inside or head-up leverage. Because of the Go's "landmark" emphasis (i.e., he knows that, first and foremost, he has to get to that wide, deep position along the sideline no matter where he lines up), his first steps will be at an angle of 45 degrees or flatter to the outside. To jam the defender will have to turn his hips to the outside to initiate and then sustain any kind of contact. Even if he is able to make contact against this type of release, two good things have happened: First, the defender will have a very hard time getting the kind of full contact jam that stops a receiver dead in his tracks and congests the route. Second, by turning his hips to work the jam, the defender has opened up the Turn area just inside him; and if he has no short help outside him, has opened up the Shoot as well. This situation is depicted in Diagram 3-25.

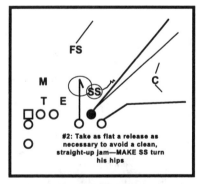

DIAGRAM 3-25
"95 TRADE" VS. SS JAM
Jam on #2 opens window for the Turn inside right inside him

"Slant" Tag for #1 in Trips Rule

If the Turn becomes a staple of your offense at all, one of the first things that will begin to happen is that, by natural reaction or design, safeties will begin tightening and closing quickly on the Turn route, trying to arrive at the same time the ball does, or at worst tackle him immediately after the catch. One good way to deal with this eventuality is to have #1 run a Slant into the void left when a safety, from either a 3-deep or 2-deep shell, recognizes and closes on the Turn. In teaching this tag, the #1 must still use an extremely wide split, and his Slant must be broken at 6 to 8 yards instead of the customary 5 to enable him to get to the void. His goal on the break is to get behind, yet stay outside of, any underneath coverage (including the reacting safety), while separating himself from the safety. The corner will most likely be playing lower with some kind of outside leverage.

The quarterback wants to help the safety along by staring down the Turn as much as possible on his initial drop, then shuffling forward to find the lane through which he will throw the deeper Slant. If he sees no lane, the ball is thrown away.

If we go into a game knowing we will face aggressive safeties, this tag will be used out of a formation from which we also plan to use a regular Turn, and we'll throw the regular Turn a couple times early to heighten the safety's recognition. Sequence and timing are important to the use of this tag, which has game-breaking potential because no one is left to tackle the Slant after the ball is caught if the offense has drawn that safety down.

Illustrations of how the Slant tag would work against two basic types of coverage follow.

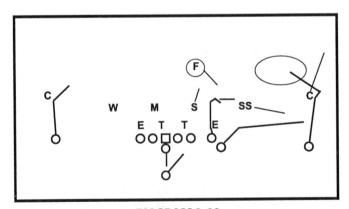

DIAGRAM 3-26
NASTY RIP PLUS 95 Z SLANT VS. COVER 3
FS low and aggressive to attack the Turn. Slant bends in
at a flatter angle because the middle is open with FS
reaction and he must separate from C

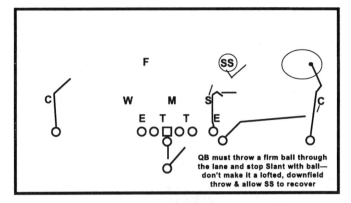

QB must throw a firm ball through the lane and stop Slant with ball— don't make it a lofted, downfield throw & allow SS to recover

DIAGRAM 3-27
NASTY RIP PLUS 95 Z SLANT VS. COVER 2
Hash safety attacks the Turn. Slant now skinnier because
less separation is needed from a low cornerback, and
safety is in closer proximity

Controlling the Second Short Defender: "Thru" and "Panther"

The defender who can most quickly disrupt the basic Turn combination is the second short defender inside the cornerback. While we are reading the first short defender, we normally expect the Turn player, through technique and the speed of the play, to beat the second one.

In cases where our matchup is not very good and the second short defender is extremely active and aggressive, we have tags we can use to control him. The first of these tags is what we call a simple "Thru" route to the back. The job of the back running the "Thru" is to simply replace that second short defender if he leaves quickly to cover the Turn. Even though negotiating the traffic to get through the line can be difficult at times, it still tends to time up well since the Thru would only come into play for the quarterback after he has looked at the Shoot/Turn combination.

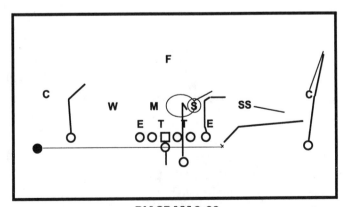

DIAGRAM 3-28
GREEN LARRY 10 X6 HOT 95 THRU
If S flies for width to bottle up the Turn, the Thru naturally
and quickly gets into the hole where he left.

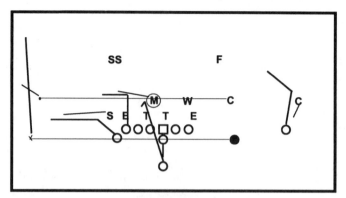

DIAGRAM 3-29
LARRY PLUS Z11 HOT 195 THRU

Another way we control the second short defender is specific to a 4-3 shell where a middle linebacker is the second short defender. In this case, which we call the "Panther" tag, we swing the fullback *away* from the Turn call to pull the linebacker backside. "Panther" also tells the backside #1 receiver to tighten his split and run a six-yard Option route. If the middle linebacker runs to the Turn anyway, the quarterback immediately goes backside, where the Option and Swing will outflank the backside linebacker 2 on 1.

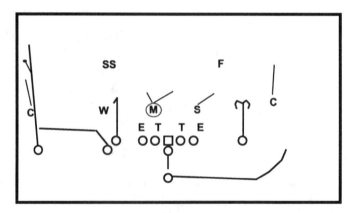

DIAGRAM 3-30
LOY PAIR HOT 195 PANTHER VS. 4-3 COVER 4
Using a weakside Swing by F to influence M away from the Turn combination. S isolated on two players if he stays strong.

The Turn Route and its Use with "Hot" Protection

Because so many of the illustrations used to this point have used "Hot" protection that enables five receivers to get into the pattern, it is important to explain why we feel so comfortable using this route while having only five protectors.

The two primary reasons Turn is such a good fit with "Hot" protection are: a) timing and b) the area which it attacks. Specifically, the speed with which the play is executed makes it difficult for even a completely free rusher to get to the passer before the ball is gone, especially because we always secure things from inside out first as a priority; therefore, any free rushers should come from the edges rather than directly up the middle.

The areas the Turn's basic routes get to on this quick timing also make it a viable "Hot" throw, since both the Turn and Shoot get to spots any unblocked rushers have vacated. Therefore, the blitz as well as the read will be directly in the quarterback's line of vision, meaning he does not have to use a separate thought process in dealing with the "hot" situation. This situation also means the receivers the quarterback will be throwing to will have big openings in which to make the catch and turn upfield.

For any "hot" route concept to work, the team should drill extensively so the quarterback and linemen understand the rusher or rushers we are leaving unblocked. For us, this practice is part of our blitz period and "hot" protection routine. We have found that this investment is well worth our time in light of all the advantages of having five receivers out for the Turn. The diagrams below show the Turn routes taking advantage of different blitzes.

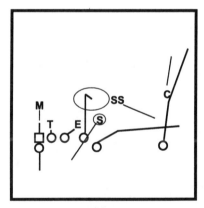

DIAGRAM 3-31
THROWING THE "TURN" ROUTE HOT OFF THE SAM LINEBACKER
Turn gets into natural hole left by S.

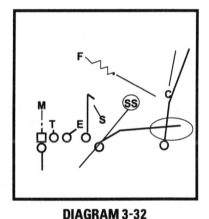

DIAGRAM 3-32
THROWING THE "TURN" ROUTE HOT OFF THE STRONG SAFETY
Shoot quickly gets to the open outside edge; FS can't break on him nearly in time.

Giving the "Turn" Route Numerous Personalities

Throughout the chapter we have alluded to and illustrated the need for Turn to be utilized from different types of personnel groupings, formations, and motion. This variety is important because the best way for a defense to neutralize the route is with a "clued in" second short defender who recognizes by formation the possibility of the Turn being run at him. The step or two this recognition gives him in aggressively attacking the inside receiver is often the difference in the route's success or failure.

Fortunately, multiplicity and flexibility are strengths of the Turn package, and once the players have learned and practiced all three parts of the frontside route in early installation, applying it to all kinds of formation structures becomes very easy. For us, having a list of five or six completely different sets from which we can run the Turn during a game is not at all unusual; it is a great aid in retarding defensive recognition.

Following are illustrations that show some of the many ways the Turn can be packaged to look different to defenses. In each of these new cases, you can see that the same learning is merely being reapplied, and the same read is used for the quarterback.

"Heavy" Three Tight End Packages

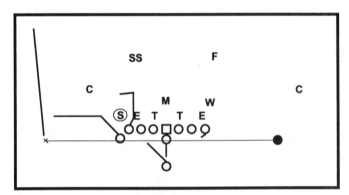

DIAGRAM 3-33
TIGHT RAM Z11 Y195 TURN

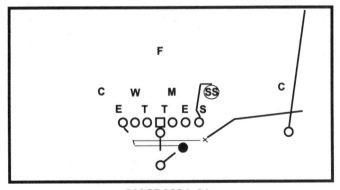

DIAGRAM 3-34
STRONG RIP TIGHT F RETURN 95 TURN

Other Two Back Varieties

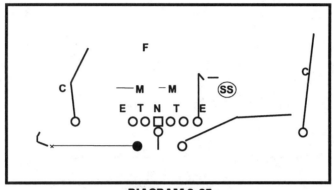

DIAGRAM 3-35
SPLIT RIP H LEFT HOT 95 SWITCH
Motion weak to create LB slide away from play

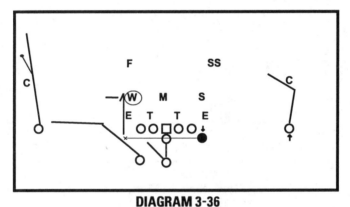

DIAGRAM 3-36
BROWN RIP Y7 195 SWITCH
Putting the Turn on the move; "stacked release" picture
given to defense with Y and H

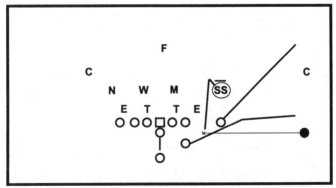

DIAGRAM 3-37
WEAK RAY X6 95 SWITCH
"Squeezed" effect—#1 works to normal "Go" landmark

Wide Sets

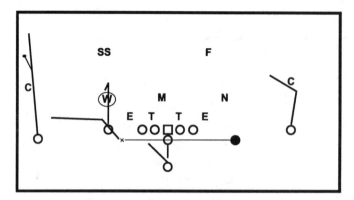

DIAGRAM 3-38
FLEX Y7 195 SWITCH

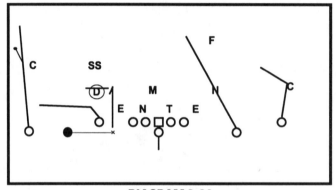

DIAGRAM 3-39
ZILCH H7 HOT 195 TURN

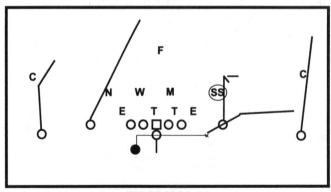

DIAGRAM 3-40
BLUE FLEX F6 HOT 95 SWITCH

Using "Bunched" sets as a decoy

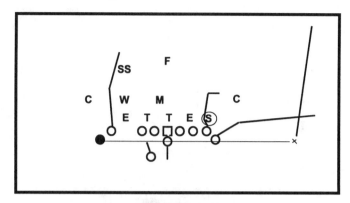

DIAGRAM 3-41
SQUEEZE BLUE LARRY OUT X10 95 TURN
3 man "Bunch" side created initially to left before motion, which
often results in a special coverage adjustment to that side;
becomes harder for defense to check to something that will get
people in good position to cover the Turn when X motions.

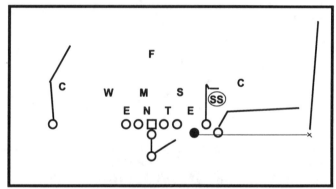

DIAGRAM 3-42
SQUEEZE REX 6 H10 95 TURN
Change-up look; SS must decide how far to widen with motion.
Any widening on his part helps create space for the Turn.

Two Receiver "Turn" Combinations Away from Trips

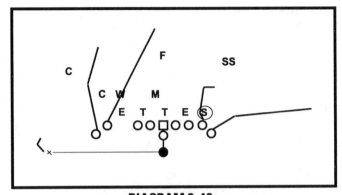

DIAGRAM 3-43
LARRY PLUS H LEFT HOT 95 TURN
Two on one away from over-rotated trips adjustment; Split
available if FS vacates deep middle for motion adjustment

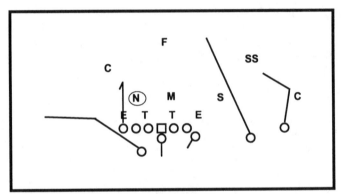

DIAGRAM 3-44
BLUE RAY HIP (BADGER) 95 SWITCH VS. COVER 3 CLOUD

Three Receiver Combinations Away from the Strong Safety

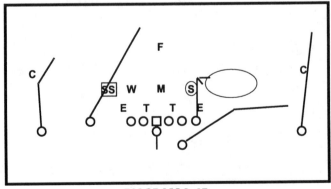

DIAGRAM 3-45
GREEN LARRY 10 HOT 95 SWITCH

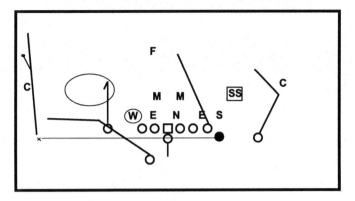

DIAGRAM 3-46
BLUE RIP PLUS F11 HOT 195 SWITCH

"Double Turn" Combinations

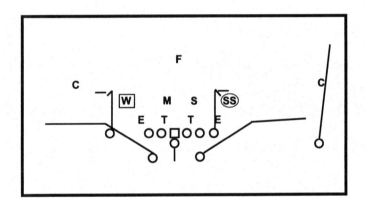

DIAGRAM 3-47
SPLIT RIP HOT 95 DOUBLE TURN (SWITCH)

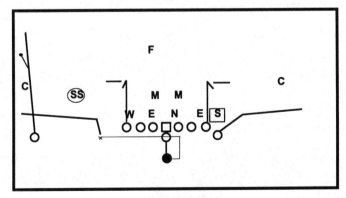

DIAGRAM 3-48
RAM WING H7 HOT 195 DOUBLE TURN

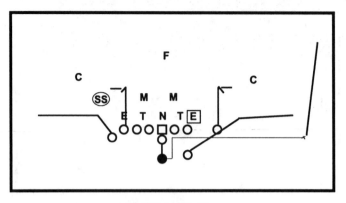

DIAGRAM 3-49
BROWN LIZ WING F10 HOT 95 SWITCH B TURN

CHAPTER 4

The "Short" Route Package

A relatively new but effective quick route that is currently being employed in the college ranks is a package we refer to as the "Short." Our first introduction to it came from Mike Emendorfer, an accomplished Offensive Coordinator at Hanover College. Coach Emendorfer has had great success with it from his spread, four-receiver sets, and after working with it during our spring practice, we found that it could have multiple uses in our system from a variety of formations, and also be tagged in different ways to give it additional dimensions.

The "Short" is a quick, ball-control, in-breaking combination that can effectively attack the underneath portion of a number of different defenses. Its basic elements are a quick, crossing type route by a wide split outside receiver (known as a "Short", hence the name for the route package) and a Slant or Slants by inside receivers. It is designed to create a horizontal stretch of the field and that stretch is used to isolate a single short defender on the Slant and the Short.

As noted, one of the "Short's" advantages is its versatility. The route's two basic elements can be geared and emphasized to attack many varied coverages in numerous situations.

First, the "Short" provides another way to use the quick passing game against "hard corner" defenses in the Cover 2 and Quarters families which are normally used to close down quick, three-step routes on the outside. Because both routes are working quickly to the inside and the defender being attacked is an *interior* defender, whether or not the corner is "soft" is irrelevant to the play.

Second, the "Short" is an excellent way to go after blitz coverage. The ideal situation against blitz coverage that brings the free safety out of the deep middle is to get a receiver quickly into that vacated area where he can enter the quarterback's vision, make a catch, and gain big yardage through the deep center of the defense. With mirrored inside Slants, the "Short" package can do just that; therefore, it is one of our leading blitz checks.

Third, the "Short" can serve on a number of levels as a man coverage beater, making it especially valuable in different parts of the Red Zone. The Slants can be deployed in a way that creates mismatches on linebackers or nickel backs, and the "Short" from the outside is trained against man coverage to rub his man off on the Slant as he leaves.

Finally, we use the "Short" to fill gaps in specialized, but important areas of our pass offense. Because of its simple read, it can be an automatic "adjustment" to certain, unexpected situations which receivers can easily get to and the quarterback can quickly read in a hurried situation. Situations of this kind include "sight adjustment" situations where a secondary player rushes from a coverage position, and "uncovered bluffs" in which we check to an uncovered call but have it taken away at the last moment.

Basic 97-197 "Short" Package Rules

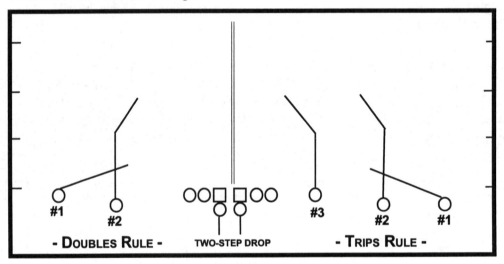

DIAGRAM 4-1
97-197 "SHORT" PACKAGE RULES

#1: Short. The receiver takes a very wide split, 16 yards as a basic rule, on the opposite numbers if he is aligned to the wide field. His job is to get to a point 3 to 4 yards deep over the original position of #2, ensuring separation from the cornerback as he does. Against a soft, zone cornerback, this positioning will entail nothing more than driving off the outside foot and angling straight to the spot. Versus a hard corner, the receiver's course should still be direct, but he may need to use a violent escape move of some sort through the corner's inside shoulder. Against a *man* corner, the receiver should use quick misdirection steps—usually "out-in-out"—make a hard head and shoulder nod outside on the last one, then drive off his outside foot and separate from the defender. The goal is to open the corner's hips or shoulders outside so the receiver can gain a clean release and a step's separation from him as he accelerates inside. Again, the receiver should prepare to swim or rip the defender's inside elbow.

The receiver should look for the ball quickly as he comes inside, being aware of the next short defender out in front of him. Against man coverage, he should keep separating and coming inside, expecting the ball out in front slightly. Against zone, the receiver is more apt to be stopped with the ball. In either case, he should be aware that the ball is coming directly at him even as he close the distance on it quickly, so it could be on top of him more quickly than he expects. He should get his hands ready and soften them, catch the ball and turn his body straight upfield immediately, gaining yardage north and south.

If he does not get the ball by the time he has reached his aiming point, particularly against zones, the receiver should work into the next hole inside the defender over #2, center himself there, and make himself available to the quarterback as a dump by making eye contact with him.

Special note: If a player is the #1 receiver on a side with no other receivers, he should run a Slant, using normal outside Slant technique. If the underneath coverage overloads the side away from him, he will get the ball.

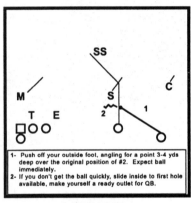

DIAGRAM 4-2
"SHORT" TECHNIQUE VS. ZONE

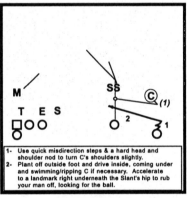

DIAGRAM 4-3
"SHORT" TECHNIQUE VS. MAN

#2: Slant. The receiver widens his normal split, using a "split the difference plus 2" rule. His job is to beat the man over him, getting into an open lane between him and the next short defender inside him. If the defender is playing with inside leverage, the receiver should threaten his outside to open his hips so he can jump inside him, then straighten up, plant and beat him to the inside on his final break. If the defender is head up, the receiver should take his best available release—inside if possible—then reestablish his original width and straighten before his final break. As he releases, if he sees any sort of Cover 2 or Cover 4 hash safety over him, the receiver should engage him in eye contact, and drive straight at him, keeping him in his backpedal. The receiver then nods at the top of his route to the outside and crosses his face to the inside.

Special note: If a receiver is the #2 player from a tight end position, he should run a "Seam."

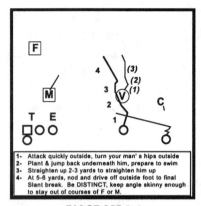

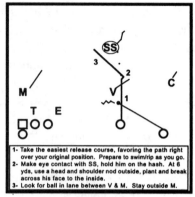

DIAGRAM 4-4
INSIDE SLANT TECHNIQUE VS. MAN

DIAGRAM 4-5
INSIDE SLANT TECHNIQUE VS.
COVER 2/4 SHELL

#3: Slant. The receiver should understand that he is controlling the short defender inside the "read" defender over #2. He should use the same Slant technique as #2, and if the short defender he is controlling crosses his face, adjust to a skinny course inside him and find the ball.

Again, a #3 receiver lined up as a tight end runs a Seam.

Quarterback: The quarterback should use a two-step drop. Generally, he chooses and works the wide side of the field unless he has a compelling reason to do otherwise. His read is the short defender over #2, and the "danger" player is the next short defender inside him. The quarterback uses his pre-snap read to determine whether the potential danger player's alignment could enable him to be a factor.

On the snap, the quarterback reads the hips and shoulders of the defender over #2. If he "hangs" over his initial position or squats on #1, the quarterback drives the Slant right through the open lane off his second step. If the defender collapses on the Slant from the outside or walls it from inside-out, the quarterback delivers a firm ball to the Short as he comes in. The quarterback should keep in mind in the latter case that the Short is running directly toward the ball, so he should not knock him down. He should deliver a firm ball on the upfield side of his neck so he can catch it easily and begin up the field.

Against man coverage, the picture the quarterback gets will give him a "Short" read, because the defender over #2 will collapse on him. If the quarterback recognizes man and thinks the Slant has a good matchup and a good lane to work in, he can wait the defender out just a bit before coming off to the Short, especially against "Blitz" man coverage with no free safety. In this case, we really want a shot to hit that Slant in the vacated middle. Throws to the Short against man coverage should *lead* him slightly and not force him to slow down.

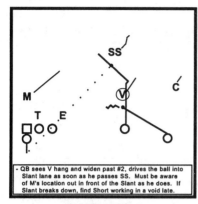

- QB sees V hang and widen past #2, drives the ball into Slant lane as soon as he passes SS. Must be aware of M's location out in front of the Slant as he does. If Slant breaks down, find Short working in a void late.

DIAGRAM 4-6
BASIC 97-197 "SHORT" READ:
DEFENDER OVER #2 HANGS

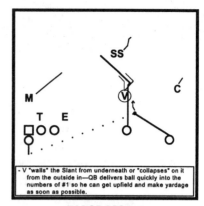

- V "walls" the Slant from underneath or "collapses" on it from the outside in—QB delivers ball quickly into the numbers of #1 so he can get upfield and make yardage as soon as possible.

DIAGRAM 4-7
BASIC 97-197 "SHORT" READ:
DEFENDER OVER #2 COLLAPSES
OR WALLS

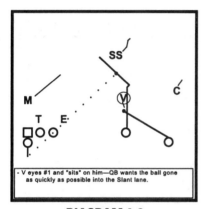

- V eyes #1 and "sits" on him—QB wants the ball gone as quickly as possible into the Slant lane.

DIAGRAM 4-8
BASIC 97-197 "SHORT" READ:
DEFENDER OVER #2 JUMPS #1

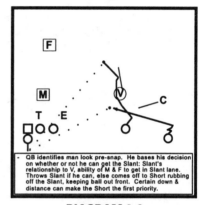

- QB identifies man look pre-snap. He bases his decision on whether or not he can get the Slant: Slant's relationship to V, ability of M & F to get in Slant lane. Throws Slant if he can, else comes off to Short rubbing off the Slant, keeping ball out front. Certain down & distance can make the Short the first priority.

DIAGRAM 4-9
BASIC 97-197 "SHORT" READ:
MAN COVERAGE

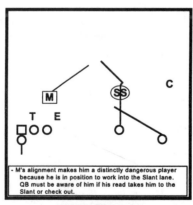

- M's alignment makes him a distinctly dangerous player because he is in position to work into the Slant lane. QB must be aware of him if his read takes him to the Slant or check out.

DIAGRAM 4-10
BASIC 97-197 "SHORT" READ:
M'S PRE-SNAP ALIGNMENT MAKES
HIM A PROBLEM

Against zones, if the quarterback gets a Slant read but something ruins it (e.g., the danger player flying into the lane, or a hash safety jumping it), he can reset his feet and come off to the Short, now an outlet, sliding in a void.

Field Width Issues

Because the Short combination relies on field spacing to isolate the defender over #2, it is largely a wide field route. The player most likely to cause the basic read difficulty is the short defender immediately inside the defender we're reading, usually an inside linebacker. When we get good receiver splits to the wide field, this defender's alignment within the front usually dictates that he will not be able to get into the Slant lane. From the middle of the field, the same principle generally applies, though the quarterback must be a little more alert to where this danger player is and where he is dropping. To the short side of the field, however, the danger player is often naturally in a position to disrupt our read. This concept is depicted below.

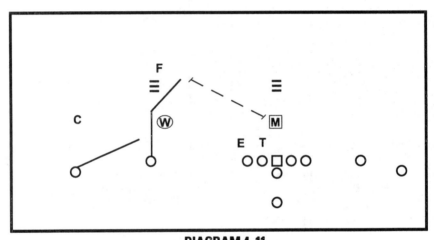

DIAGRAM 4-11
SHORT COMBINATION TO THE WIDE FIELD
**W effectively isolated; M can't become a factor because
the field width gives him too much ground to cover.**

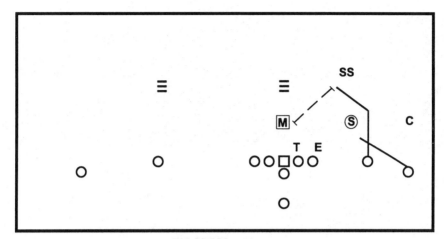

DIAGRAM 4-12
SHORT COMBINATION INTO THE BOUNDARY
**S not effectively isolated, because short distance M has
to travel enables him to be a factor in the Slant lane.**

Most often, if we are calling a balanced, 2 x 2 "Short" from one hash or another, we use a special call to give the receivers into the boundary a different combination so the quarterback has something to work with if he does not like the Short to the wide field. The tool that allows us to do this is called the "B" tag; it is discussed and illustrated fully in Volume 3 Chapter 2.

Special Uses for the "Short"

As we mentioned earlier, the simplicity and quickness of the Short's development make it useful in a number of situations. Two such situations we use it for are as a sight adjustment against a secondary blitz and as a "recovery" mechanism when a team bluffs us into making an uncovered call and then takes the uncovered receiver away. We make use of other simple combinations in sight adjusting and uncovered recovery as well, based on game plan, but Short has been one of our most effective. Its use in these instances is shown below.

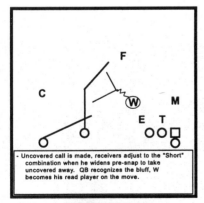

DIAGRAM 4-13
**"SHORT" COMBINATION AS AN
ADJUSTMENT TO AN
UNCOVERED BLUFF**

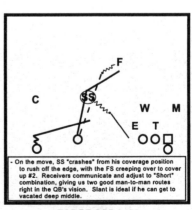

DIAGRAM 4-14
**"SHORT" COMBINATION AS A BLITZ
SIGHT ADJUSTMENT**

Attacking Coverages with the Short
Cover 1 Blitz

Because of its ability to strike quickly down the middle where blitz coverage leaves, Short is one of our best calls or checks against Cover 1 Blitz. The quarterback's read, because of man coverage, will likely tell him to go to the Short, since he'll see the defender over #2 collapse; however, he should, by pre-snap read, be able to spot the fact that a blitz coverage is occurring. In this situation he will "wait out" the Slant as long as he can, hoping the receiver will beat his man and get to that deep middle. If the Slant breaks open, the quarterback should continue to lead him upfield as much as possible, and get the ball over linebackers in front. He also must be aware of secondary players who have been "freed up" by their man blocking who might drift into position in front of the Slant.

If the Slant gets held up or encounters some kind of problem from the inside, the Short should be available crossing from outside in.

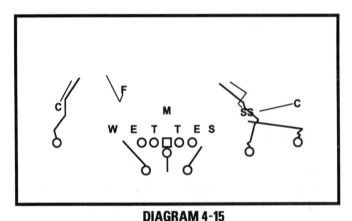

DIAGRAM 4-15
SPLIT REX 97 SHORT VS. COVER 1 BLITZ
**Inside Slant has a chance to make a big play down the vacated
deep middle area.**

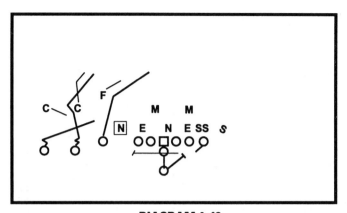

DIAGRAM 4-16
LARRY 11 (COLT) 197 SHORT VS. COVER 1 BLITZ
Two Slants have a chance to beat man coverage and exploit the
lack of a free safety. Short by H has a great chance in certain
situations because he's cutting underneath two potential rubs.
"Colt" call moves F to backside protection to account for SS
blitz, enabling "hot" throw to happen off N, which is in the QB's
vision. F can also work back to left if no backside blitz shows.

Cover 1 Free

One of the Short's real advantages against man coverage is that it enables us to
isolate two receivers in space against two defenders who can not get much help on
the two routes we are running. Normally, the wide field precludes the defenders
from getting help from the inside, and they can not get help from each other
because the two inside breaks make switching impossible.

Which part of the combination we want to emphasize determines how we will line
up in running the Short against Cover 1 Free. If we want to throw to the Slant and
come off to the Short later, we will try to create physical mismatches on the inside.
If we are emphasizing the Short, we will try to gain quickness mismatches on the
outside and use sets that make full use of "rubs" for the outside man. Diagram 4-17
illustrates an instance of setting things up for the Slant, Diagram 4-18 shows an
example of us emphasizing the Short, and Diagram 4-19 depicts a case where we
could feasibly go to either.

Diagram 4-20 is also a case where either receiver might be available, depending on
who the opponent is. In this illustration, motion is used to cause leverage problems
for the defender bumping down to cover the Short. The motioning Slant may also
find himself with a softer shoulder to attack in releasing against his man, making it
easier to beat him to the inside.

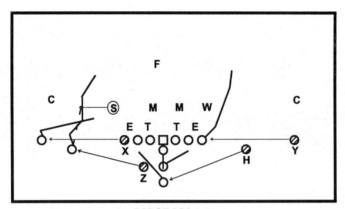

DIAGRAM 4-17
SHIFT TO LARRY 197 SHORT VS. 4-4 COVER 1 FREE
Special shift used to lock slower Sam linebacker into coverage on Z running Slant against a 4-4 defense.

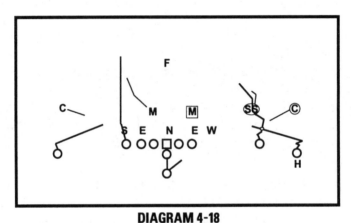

DIAGRAM 4-18
LIZ 10 97 SHORT VS. COVER 1 FREE
M's location probably means that the QB will work to the Short, rubbing under the Slant. "10" alignment by H makes him the Short runner, creating excellent R.A.C. possibilities.

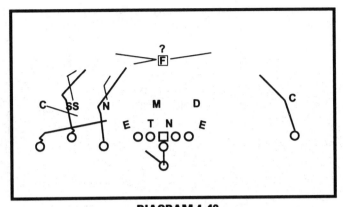

DIAGRAM 4-19
LEX 7 197 SHORT VS. COVER 1 FREE
Free safety has three Slants to worry about—must decide which
to commit to. Short has two Slants to rub off of underneath.

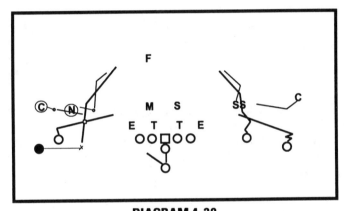

DIAGRAM 4-20
RON 11 H9 197 SHORT VS. "BUMPED" COVER 1 FREE
C's motion adjustment leaves him with poor leverage on
Short, who also gets a quick rub off of the motioning Slant.
May also create a mismatch on the Slant.

Cover 2

Cover 2 is the coverage for which this route was originally installed in our offense because most 4-3, Cover 2 teams will end up with a middle linebacker as the potential "danger" player, and his alignment over the center effectively means that either outside linebacker (or nickel back) is isolated in space against the Slant and Short. Again, the corner is really no factor in the play at all; even if he tries to jam and funnel #1 hard, he will shove him right into his normal route course.

Our basic philosophy in running the Short against Cover 2 is to use sets that spread the zone defenders as wide as possible. This spread further isolates the people over #2 from inside help, widens the safeties, and creates bigger running lanes for our receivers after the catch.

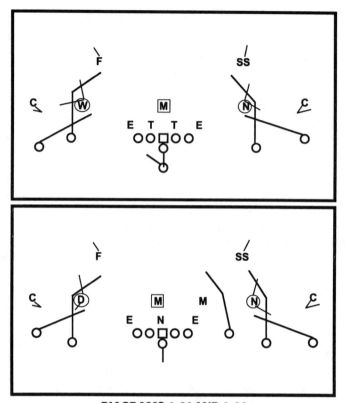

DIAGRAMS 4-21 AND 4-22
FLEX 197 SHORT (TOP) & EMPTY 97 OR 197 SHORT (BOTTOM)
Spreading out Cover 2 to isolate defenders over #2 on each side.
QB can pick a side based on matchups or best-located inside LB.

Cover 3

While the Short can certainly be effective against Cover 3, a distinct precaution must be taken in its use. Cover 3 often has an inside linebacker in a much better position to be a "danger" player than does Cover 2 or Cover 4. This alignment is shown below.

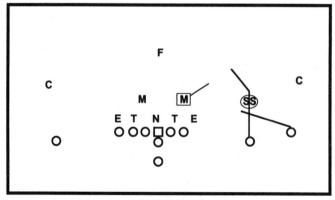

DIAGRAM 4-23
97 SHORT FROM A 2 X 2 SET VS. COVER 3
M is in a position to be a danger player.

At times, based on scouting reports or because of field width, we can still get away with a basic 2 x 2 Short combination. As long as we are certain that the linebacker will not work underneath the Slant and destroy the basic read, we do not have a problem. Generally, however, we prefer to control this man by employing a "trips rule" Short combination, allowing us to hit #3's Slant right inside this linebacker if he opens up for too much width.

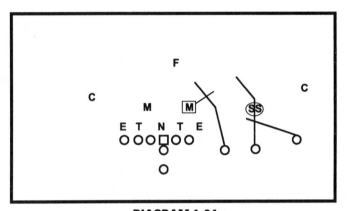

DIAGRAM 4-24
97 SHORT FROM A 3 X 1 SET VS. COVER 3
Third receiver running Slant used to control M if he widens to
cause problems for basic read.

The tight end as #3 can also serve the same purpose running his Seam, particularly if the potential danger player is lined up inside him. In these cases, we are much less apt to throw to #3 since the danger player will usually "wall" him.

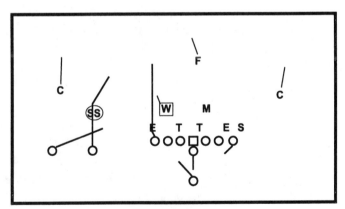

DIAGRAM 4-25
RAM Z   Y197 SHORT VS. COVER 3
Using TE's "Seam rule" to hold off next short defender; SS
isolated in space on Short/Slant

Cover 4

Our approach to using the Short against Cover 4 is very similar to the way we use it to attack Cover 2, since the underneath structures are the same. We do, however, have two concerns we must deal with that are different with Cover 4.

The first of these concerns relates to the play of the safeties. They will not necessarily change the reading process for us, but many Cover 4 safeties play much "tighter," really trying to attack vertical releases from the inside. The inside Slant must be prepared to "bend, swim, and straighten" as he approaches this kind of safety. "Bending" means he will flatten his course a bit after a nod to jump underneath the safety, then be prepared to swim or rip his inside elbow as he goes by. When he "straightens," then, he is essentially "on top" of or "restacked" over this safety and can now fully separate from him.

The second concern deals with how the quarterback sees the read develop. Because many Cover 4 outside linebackers are schooled to "wall" the vertical release of #2 and then "break on" #1 when they see him come inside, the read tends to happen at a different pace. As we practice it, the quarterback can do one of two things: he can "speed the read up" or "slow it down." Which technique we use depends on our quarterback, receivers, and the specific technique of the individual defenders. If the quarterback "speeds the read up," he will try to drive the Short in quickly, before the linebacker can come off #2 and get in position to defend the Short. This situation is probably the more likely of the two scenarios because the "wall and break" technique we are describing isn't easy, and the man executing it has a long way to go.

If the quarterback "slows the read down," he waits for the linebacker to disengage the Slant and come off to the Short, opening the Slant lane. This maneuver can involve a bit of gamesmanship on the quarterback's part, including a "shoulder fake" out to the Short, in which he twists and opens his shoulders briefly as though he is going to the wide man. If you find defenses that key the quarterback's shoulders, as some do, this method is an effective way to guarantee the Slant.

Of course, we see plenty of Cover 4 teams against whom this read is not a factor since they do not "wall and break." In these cases, the read looks and functions just as it would against Cover 2. It is important, however, that a team be aware of its possibility and its implications for the quarterback.

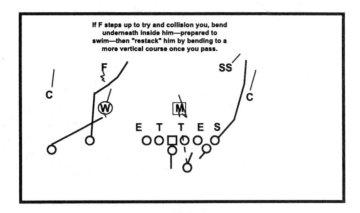

DIAGRAM 4-26
GREEN LARRY IN (COLT) 197 SHORT VS. COVER 4
Basic Short read off W with #2 adjusting his route if F really sits
on him. "Green" call used to create a potential three man
"bunch" to the right, influencing M a step or two that way. W,
the read player, becomes hot, so protection isn't a problem. If he
rushes, he must declare early because of #2's wide alignment,
and the Short will be open instantly in the area he vacated.

Special Tags and Adjustments

"Flow"

The first special adjustment we will discuss involves a simple backfield action that we use to try to control the "danger" player. If we see that interior linebackers key backfield action hard, we can use a protection wrinkle called "Flow" that sends both backs on a course left, taking the inside linebackers that way. Even if they are keying through the quarterback and see him backing up on a normal drop, the sight of the backs quickly going away should at least freeze them for a step.

The first of the "flowing" backs assumes protection responsibility to the side he is going, meaning the protection essentially functions as though it has been "Badgered." Nothing changes at all for the quarterback except that his job is easier since the danger player has been accounted for by the action.

This adjustment can be useful against any coverage as long as the linebackers key the backfield action. Against man coverage it is especially effective, since those linebackers will be forced to run with their coverage responsibility.

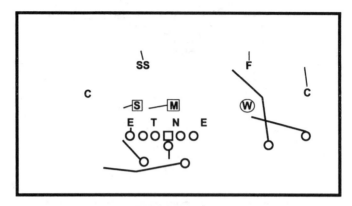

DIAGRAM 4-27
SPLIT RAY (FLOW) Y97 SHORT VS. COVER 4
Using special full-flow backfield action to move M who keys
backs hard. Isolation on W, who's "hot" by protection, results.

"Swing"

The first and simplest tag we will install to complement the Short is a simple
"Swing" out of the backfield. Generally, this tag is used against a flat defender who
wants to try to cause problems for the read with a hard collision of his man,
creating a big pile of people in his vicinity. In general, we do not think this collision
should ever happen to one of our receivers, since we are extremely committed to
release work, but the "Swing" gives us something to go to in case it happens. Should
the read defender try to jam in this fashion, the Swing will get outside him, catch
the ball, and be gaining yards upfield before he can get to him.

Aside from this very specific purpose, the Swing can function as a good general-
purpose outlet. It can also be used through motion to create a stretch of underneath
coverage in a zone before they are ready to stretch.

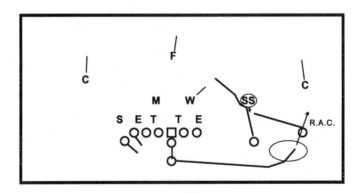

DIAGRAM 4-28
RAY PLUS STAY 97 SWING VS. COVER 3
"Swing" takes advantage of flat defenders over #2 who
try to blow up the play by collisioning the Slant. Swing tag
can also control "jam and close" Cover 2 corners as shown
in 4-29, or serve as a solid, all-purpose "dump."

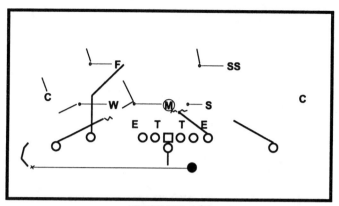

DIAGRAM 4-29
GREEN LARRY 10 F LEFT HOT 197 SWING Y SIT VS. COVER 4
Swing used to create a stretch of the defense through motion,
creates imbalance quickly. When W, sliding, passes #2, M
becomes the read player. The effect of motion makes it very
difficult for the defense to get an additional LB into a position to
stop the Slant—in this case it would have to be S. "Sit" by Y used
to control S. Slant could break open down the middle if SS & FS
are late or poorly coordinated in their motion adjustment.

"Corner"

The next of the tags is a "Corner" tag for the #2 receiver. We will use this tag specifically in sequence throughout a game with our basic 97, especially against teams who do a good job recognizing patterns and making adjustments. When we tell #2 to run a "Corner," we are essentially telling him to run the same route and use the same technique as he would on a "Quick Smash" (see Chapter 1).

The Corner tag has two general uses. First, against any type of man coverage, the receiver will be running to completely open space against a man defender once the Short draws his man inside. Again, good mismatches can be created by lining up our Z against a defense's strong safety or nickel back.

The second use of this tag is against a Cover 2 corner really intent on his "jam and close" technique, riding the Short all the way down inside as he recognizes the release and the fact that he has no flat threat. In this case, the Corner receiver will have a big hole to run to outside and behind the defender. "Corner" sequences well with the basic route against the safety as well, since he is used to seeing #2 try to cross his face to the Slant.

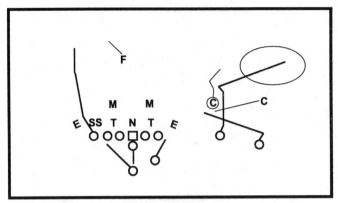

DIAGRAM 4-30
WEAK RAY 97 CORNER VS. COVER 1
Z matched against an inside leverage man defender, can use the
wide field to accelerate away when C runs inside with the
Short. QB must use a lofted throw and let Z run under it, not
breaking stride as he separates from the defender.

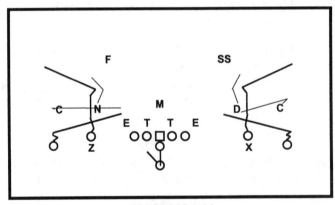

DIAGRAM 4-31
LOU 10 197 DOUBLE CORNER VS. COVER 2 MAN
Flipping wide receivers inside to create better matchups for the
routes to the Corner. Both should have a good chance because
they can use DBs' inside leverage against them; they must push
straight at safeties for 4 yards, keeping them in their backpedals.
QB favors the wide field side with all things equal, throws like a
Quick Smash. "Short" still a viable option off a rub in shorter
down and distance situations.

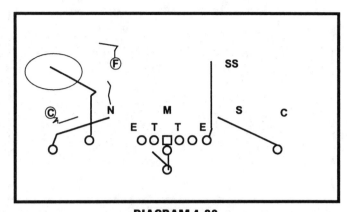

DIAGRAM 4-32
RIP 9 197 CORNER VS. COVER 2 WITH "JAM & CLOSE" CORNERS
Cornerback who jams and rides the Short down inside to disrupt the
route's read opens hole for "Corner" behind him. Also sequences well
vs. hash safety who's used to seeing Slant try to cross his face.

The "Plant"

Another of our tags to the "Short" route is an adjustment to #2 we call "Plant."
Essentially, a "Plant" is no more than a basic Hitch route extended to 8 yards with a
slightly more outside weave.

In running the Plant, we are still reading the same defender, the man over #2, and by
squeezing the #1 receiver into closer proximity to the Plant, we hope to turn the
defender inside with the Short, opening up the Plant behind him. If he walls off the
Plant instead, the Short has an extremely good chance for a good run after the
catch, since the Plant's increased depth forces the man over him to wall longer,
meaning he will come off to tackle the Short later.

The "Plant" can also be very effective when used with a "Swing" tag, because the
Swing has a tendency to pull the flat defender with it and open up the Plant inside
it.

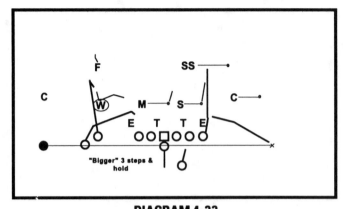

DIAGRAM 4-33
GREEN LARRY PAIR X10 (BADGER) 197 PLANT VS. COVER 4
Motion and offset back used to create movement by M away
from the read. QB works off isolated W, hits the Short
quickly if he walls/hangs, or the "Plant" if he widens past #2
or turns inside with the Short.

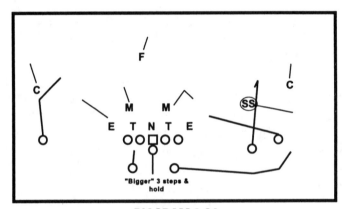

DIAGRAM 4-34
SPLIT ROY 97 PLANT H SWING VS. COVER 3
Pulling flat coverage with the Swing to open up the Plant.

The "Seam"

Earlier in the chapter, we discussed the fact that, because of the linebacker
positioning it often entails, Cover 3 can pose a problem for us in throwing the "Short"
route from 2 x 2 sets. One way we can deal with this issue is by giving the #2
receiver a "Seam," which keeps him on a course wide enough to stay out of the
danger linebacker's drop.

In using this maneuver, we change nothing in the quarterback's read, and we use a
throw he is already used to executing from the 91, 92, and 94 route packages. If the
man over #2 "walls" or stays inside the Seam, the ball is delivered to the Short in
the void that remains. If the man over #2 widens, the quarterback drives the ball
into the Seam route right on time just as he would in the other "Seam Read" routes
mentioned above.

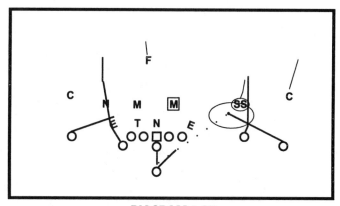

DIAGRAM 4-35
L 8 97 SEAM VS. COVER 3 - MAN OVER #2 RUNS WITH SEAM
Seam route makes it much more difficult for danger player, **M**, to
get into lane of #2's route. Good North and South running lane for
the Short after the catch if SS works underneath the Seam
vertically.

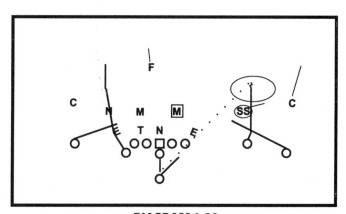

DIAGRAM 4-36
L 8 97 SEAM VS. COVER 3 - MAN OVER #2 WORKS FOR WIDTH
Seam route makes it much more difficult for danger player, **M**, to
get into lane of #2's route. SS's course "opens the door" for the
Seam, which is delivered on time into the void.

CHAPTER 5

The Picks: "In" and "Out" Route Packages

The "In" and the "Out" are two specifically packaged routes designed to create separation against man coverage. We refer to them as our "picks" because the complementary routes and rules we surround them with are identical, and we always designate one player to act as a "picker," who creates an impediment for the man covering the In and the Out, or a "rub."

When the routes were originally created, they were integrated into a "no back" package, and the complementary routes were designed to make use of five receiver sets and work with five-man protection to get people into certain, easily accessible places in case of the blitz.

We have since broadened the use of the In and Out for use with more types of sets, but have kept the original package rules in place. The focus of the chapter is not the entirety of the route package so much as it is the specific ways that an "In" or "Out" route can be teamed with a "picker" to attack coverages. You can easily set up routes around the In or Out combinations that you think are easiest for your players to learn or that suit your needs best; the basic concept of attack will still hold up.

Basic Attack Concept of the "In" and "Out" Combinations

The basic idea behind the In and the Out is to use two receivers in a choreographed fashion to rub the defender over our "target" player (the man running the In or Out) with our designated "picker." The target player should set his defender up so that his hips are actually forced to turn opposite the direction of the final break. The target player then times his break in such a way that he rubs himself just underneath the picker as he passes. Timed and executed correctly, the defender over the target receiver will turn his hips and recover just in time to be impeded by the picker, and either collide with him or be forced to "bubble" around him. The defender over the picker, whether in man or zone coverage, should have to open his hips to run with the picker, enabling the target receiver to get underneath him as he clears the rub.

The quarterback should time his delivery in such a way that the ball gets into the hands of the target just as he clears the rub. This delivery minimizes the time that either defender has to recover. Rhythm is a vital part of the play.

Because of the timing and the effect that is being created on the defense, each of these plays has an excellent chance of a tremendous run after catch; the target receiver is accelerating and separating directly away from two different defenders into open space of some sort.

The way these routes are run dictates that they are generally best against either man coverages (and most any man variation) or zones whose underneath defenders are very active in running with routes within their zones. The routes can also, at times, be effective against "spot-drop" zones, especially those with only four defenders underneath, but we generally prefer them against man or active zones.

Basic Package Rules
In building our "In" and "Out" packages, we start with default rules that players follow unless they are tagged otherwise. These rules relate to a receiver's relative position within the formation and whether he is to or away from the call side ("In" and "Out" are not "mirrored" front and backside as most of our other quick routes are). The "default" rules are illustrated in Diagram 5-1.

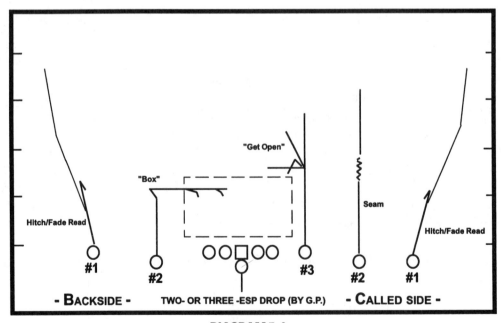

DIAGRAM 5-1
STARTING POINT ASSIGNMENTS FOR "IN" AND "OUT" PACKAGES

It is from this base that we make "In" and "Out" calls. Whenever we tell a certain receiver to run one of these routes by saying, for example, "90 Z In," or "190 H Out," another receiver next to the receiver tagged knows he must serve as a "picker." In the case of an "In" call, the player immediately *inside* the tagged receiver picks, and on an "Out" call, the next player *outside* is the picker. All other receivers in the pattern apply their base rules. The #1 receiver away from the call has a Hitch/Fade read, #2 away from the call has a "Box" route, and any frontside receivers not involved with the picking combination will either run their standard "Get Open" (if he is the #3 receiver and #1 and #2 are involved in the In/Out combination), or a "Hitch/ Fade Read" (if he is the #1 receiver and #2 and #3 are involved in the In/Out combination).

Different examples of how these rules apply are shown below. Note that in the case of #3 having the "Out" (Diagram 5-5), the #1 receiver must apply his "sandbox principle" (see Volume 3 Appendix F) and run the Fade part of his Hitch/Fade read to avoid close proximity to the "Out" receiver.

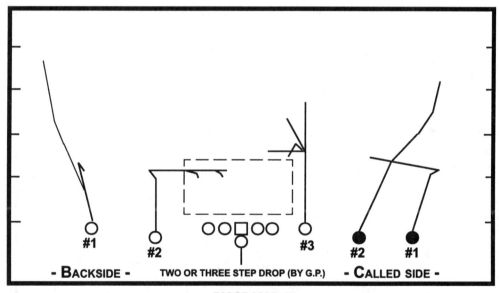

DIAGRAM 5-2
#1 ON CALLED SIDE TAGGED TO RUN "IN", #2 IS NEXT INSIDE AND MUST BECOME "PICKER", EVERYONE ELSE KEEPS DEFAULT ASSIGNMENTS.

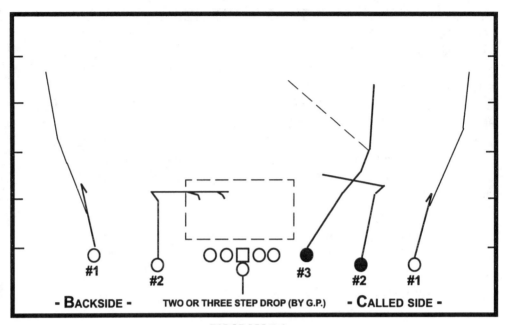

DIAGRAM 5-3
#2 TAGGED TO RUN "IN," #3 MUST NOW BECOME THE PICKER. EVERYONE ELSE HAS DEFAULT PACKAGE RULES.

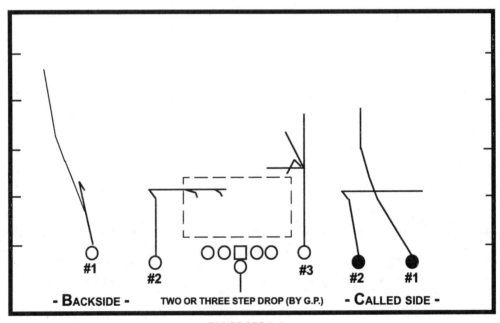

DIAGRAM 5-4
#2 ON CALLED SIDE TAGGED TO RUN AN "OUT"—#1 IS NEXT OUTSIDE HIM AND MUST BECOME THE "PICKER." EVERYONE ELSE RUNS NORMAL DEFAULT RULE.

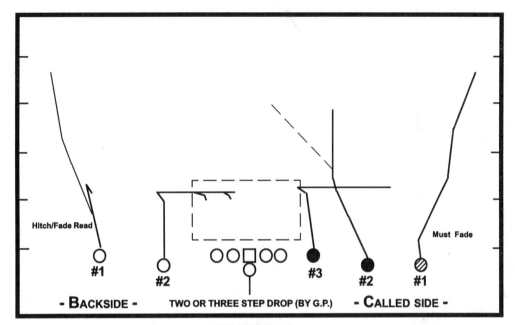

Hitch/Fade Read

Must Fade

#1   #2   #3   #2   #1

- BACKSIDE -   TWO OR THREE STEP DROP (BY G.P.)   **- CALLED SIDE -**

DIAGRAM 5-5
**#3 RECEIVER TAGGED TO RUN "OUT"—#2 IS NEXT OUTSIDE AND MUST
BECOME THE PICKER. #1, ON HIS HITCH/FADE READ, <u>MUST</u> FADE BECAUSE
A HITCH WOULD VIOLATE THE OUT'S "SANDBOX."**

Special Case: Three Receivers Away from the Call

It does not happen often, but in some cases we use all five eligible receivers, and call the "In" or "Out" combination to the two receiver side, leaving 3 receivers on the side away from the call. Since we do not have a default backside #3 rule, we have to create a special "exception" rule. The basic premise we follow is to always have the inside most player away from the play working the "Box" so the quarterback has someone working toward him. He can quickly go if there is a blitz or the basic combination breaks down. We also, however, want someone to be able to take advantage of a deep middle with no free safety, which the "Get Open" route can do. Following this logic, on a trips side away from an In or Out call, the #3 receiver, being the inside most backside receiver, will run a "Box," and the player just outside him (#2) will run the "Get Open" over top. The backside #1's rule doesn't change. Again, depending on how much time you want to give the In/Out package in your total offense, you may not want to deal with the learning needed to use this kind of exception, and thus never use the In or Out away from three receivers. In our case, it has proven worthwhile and valuable. An illustration of this "exception" follows.

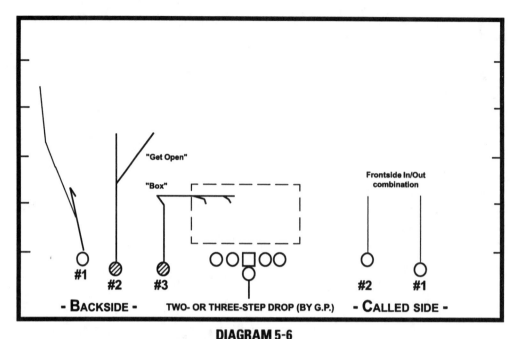

DIAGRAM 5-6
SPECIAL CASE: THREE RECEIVERS AWAY FROM CALLED SIDE. INSIDE MOST STILL HAS THE "BOX," #2 HAS THE "GET OPEN" OVER TOP OF HIM. MUST CHOOSE ONE OF TWO DEEPER OPTIONS TO STAY CLEAR OF #3'S SANDBOX.

Basic In and Out Component Route Rules and QB Reads

Hitch/Fade Read. The receiver should use a *wide* split, maximizing the space between him and the defense's interior. His basic alignment should be 14 yards outside the tackle or tight end on his side. He attacks the corner to the outside on his initial weave, reading the defender's feet. Unless the defender's feet are stopped at six yards or less or closing up on him, the receiver executes good "Hitch" technique, breaking at six yards. With good arm drive, he threatens the corner deep and gets him out of his backpedal. The receiver plants on his outside foot and snaps his head and shoulders to the inside, hands ready for the ball. He should plant and snap into the break, not wander or roll.

If the corner does close or level at 6 or less, the receiver should keep attacking to the outside shoulder, swim him outside, and convert to a Fade.

If #3 to his side is tagged with the "Out," the receiver must Fade.

"Box." The receiver is free to get open anywhere within the "Box," basically an area extending one yard beyond each tackle and seven yards deep. He must provide two things for the quarterback: first, a place he can quickly go to beat the blitz or very quick pressure; and second, an easily found outlet that is open and has made eye contact with him late if the basic read breaks down.

Against zone coverage, the receiver basically wants to push up straight to a depth of five or six yards, break inside, and sit in the first available zone window. He should show his numbers to the quarterback and feel the presence of the man out in front of him, staying centered between this defender and the defender behind him. If the man in front of the receiver works toward him very actively, he should slide under him and get to the next hole beyond his drop.

Against man coverage, the receiver should work to turn the hips of the man over him to the outside. Once he does he should jump back underneath him, straighten for at least 2-3 yards, nod outside, and make a distinct, flat break across. If the defender stays underneath the receiver and the receiver can not get inside, he should release over the top, make a great misdirection move at the top of his break (5 to 6 yards deep), and break flat over the top of the defender. In either case, the key against man coverage is to separate.

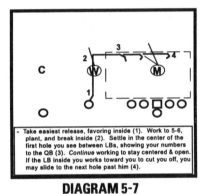

DIAGRAM 5-7
"BOX" ROUTE VS. ZONE COVERAGE

- Take easiest release, favoring inside (1). Work to 5-6, plant, and break inside (2). Settle in the center of the first hole you see between LBs, showing your numbers to the QB (3). *Continue* working to stay centered & open. If the LB inside you works toward you to cut you off, you may slide to the next hole past him (4).

DIAGRAM 5-8
"BOX" ROUTE VS. MAN COVERAGE

- Work to turn the hips of your man outside (1), then jump underneath him (2). Once underneath, straighten up 2-3 yds, nod at a depth of 6, plant, and break inside, accelerate on a flat course (3). If he won't let you inside, work over top of him, nodding and accelerating (A). Be alert for free defenders lurking in front as you cross (4).

Picker (In): The receiver releases on a course that will take him right through the inside leg of the man over the In. As this man widens, the receiver adjusts his course so he stays lined up on his inside leg until the last possible moment. Against zone, he makes his course look as much like a flat-type break as possible to bring the man over him to the outside with him. As the course of the defender he is picking begins to approach his, the receiver slows down to force the defender to run either through or around him. If a collision occurs, the receiver should run through it with his eyes up and his arms pumping. After the "rub" point, he straightens up deep on a course similar to a Fade, versus banjos, and keeps inside leverage on the cornerback.

In: The receiver comes off the ball a bit slower than normal and under control, working to set up the picker. He should "tease" his man outside, trying to get him to turn his hips that way, and make a harder nod outside at 5 to 6 yards. At 6, after making his nod, the receiver should plant and time his break to come right off the hip of the picker as he passes. Against tighter techniques, the receiver may "whirl" underneath himself if he feels it helps his break. He should expect the ball immediately and break at any angle that gets him to the most "clean air," understanding that flatter angles are generally safest.

Versus a Cover 2 or Cover 4 shell, the receiver should see and feel the linebacker over the picker, and be prepared to catch the ball on either side of him.

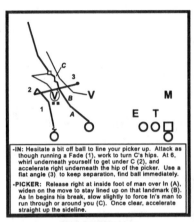

-IN: Hesitate a bit off ball to line your picker up. Attack as though running a Fade (1), work to turn C's hips. At 6, whirl underneath yourself to get under C (2), and accelerate right underneath the hip of the picker. Use a flat angle (3) to keep separation, find ball immediately.

-PICKER: Release right at inside foot of man over In (A), widen on the move to stay lined up on that landmark (B). As In begins his break, slow slightly to force In's man to run through or around you (C). Once clear, accelerate straight up the sideline.

DIAGRAM 5-9
"IN" COMBINATION TECHNIQUE
VS. TIGHT MAN COVERAGE

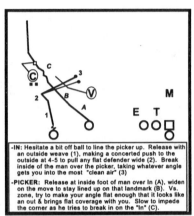

-IN: Hesitate a bit off ball to line the picker up. Release with an outside weave (1), making a concerted push to the outside at 4-5 to pull any flat defender wide (2). Break inside of the man over the picker, taking whatever angle gets you into the most "clean air" (3)

-PICKER: Release at inside foot of man over In (A), widen on the move to stay lined up on that landmark (B). Vs. zone, try to make your angle flat enough that it looks like an out & brings flat coverage with you. Slow to impede the corner as he tries to break in on the "In" (C).

DIAGRAM 5-10
"IN" COMBINATION TECHNIQUE VS.
SOFT CORNER AND/OR ZONE

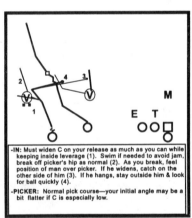

-IN: Must widen C on your release as much as you can while keeping inside leverage (1). Swim if needed to avoid jam, break off picker's hip as normal (2). As you break, feel position of man over picker. If he widens, catch on the other side of him (3). If he hangs, stay outside him & look for ball quickly (4).

-PICKER: Normal pick course—your initial angle may be a bit flatter if C is especially low.

DIAGRAM 5-11
"IN" COMBINATION TECHNIQUE
VS. COVER 2/4 SHELL

Picker (Out): The receiver's basic mechanics are like the "In" picker's, only reversed. He should attack the *outside* leg of the man over the Out, continuing to mirror that course, and slow to make himself an obstacle as that man tries to break on the Out. Against zones, the receiver may work a step upfield to try to draw the man over him down as well.

Once the rub has occurred, the receiver straightens and accelerates, understanding he could get the ball immediately if everyone widens with the out. He should stay in a wide "tube," out of the free safety's reach.

Out: The receiver teases his man to the inside, trying to turn his hips inside. At 5-6 yards, he gives a final, hard inside nod, plants on his inside foot and drives outside right off the picker's hip. He should be flat and not gain depth. The receiver should find the ball immediately, then go get the sideline and turn upfield.

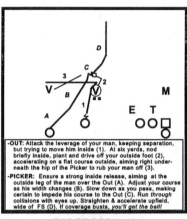

DIAGRAM 5-12
"OUT" COMBINATION TECHNIQUE
VS. MAN COVERAGE

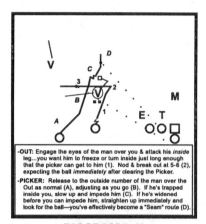

DIAGRAM 5-13
"OUT" COMBINATION TECHNIQUE
VS. ZONE COVERAGE

Quarterback: The quarterback should take three steps and hold, using his eyes initially to go from the free safety to identifying any danger players under or in front of his target player. In this way, he will keep himself out of trouble and also avoid "staring down" his route. Unless a special coverage situation dictates otherwise, he should time his throw to hit the target man right out of his break, just as he clears the picker. If the basic read does not materialize, the quarterback should reset his hips immediately to find the "Box" route as an outlet. He should never throw into a crowded lane, but understand he has this Box as a safe dump.

Exceptions to the basic read would include a Cover 2 or 4 shell versus the In, zones in general versus the Out, or a banjoed man technique versus either route. Against Cover 2 or 4 when throwing the In, the quarterback should specifically read the man over the picker. If he "hangs," the quarterback hits the In immediately on the outside of him. If he opens his hips and widens, the quarterback waits for the In to clear him, hitting him on the inside of this defender.

If the quarterback is throwing the Out against zones, he should understand that it will work much like the "Seam/Out" read on the Fade/Out combination. If he feels underneath coverage widening with the Out, he should drive the ball into the Seam hole to the picker clearing right behind.

Against banjos, the quarterback should peek at the man over the target player to see if he hesitates or stops his feet; if he does, the quarterback should feel it and go up top to the picker. Otherwise, he executes his normal throw to the target man.

Attacking Coverages with "In" and "Out" Variations
"Locked" Man Coverage

The rubs naturally created by "In" and "Out" make them one of the three or four best routes in our entire offense against man coverage. Our thought process in attacking "locked" man coverage with these routes is to either force a bad match-up for the defense by locking a strong safety or linebacker on our "target" receiver, or use a "big body" as the picker to make him difficult to work around (or through) for defenders. Often, this "big body" is a tight end of some kind.

One special way we have of trying to guarantee the best match-up is to use a "motion check" for the target player. We will start our ultimate target player in the backfield and create a cadence call for the quarterback that motions him one way or the other, depending on which direction gives him the best match-up. The motion call will also tell the rest of the players which side is frontside, who blocks, who picks, and so forth. The quarterback will be given a very specific criteria (e.g., motion him away from the free safety) for sending him, depending on how the defense adjusts to motion. Our "Ram" set is ideal for using this tool.

Another means of maximizing our match-up is to put a fast player inside, a player like our Z or H receiver, and match him up on a linebacker or a nickel back on the "Out" combination. If we can deliver the ball on time and not slow him down, he has an excellent chance to come off the rub, accelerate away, and make yards after the catch.

Read-wise, we count on the quarterback to account for any defender "out in front" of the target receiver with his peripheral vision as he makes his drop. We feel as though the picking combination will take care of the two defenders over the target receiver and picker; we need to be concerned about "stray" defenders who do not have a man coverage responsibility and make sure they do not work into our throwing lane.

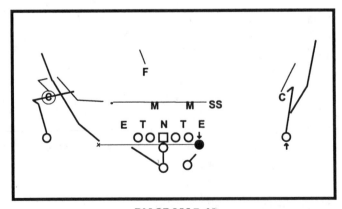

DIAGRAM 5-14
BROWN RIP Y9 190 X IN VS. MAN COVERAGE
Motioning Y used as a "big picker" for X's In route.

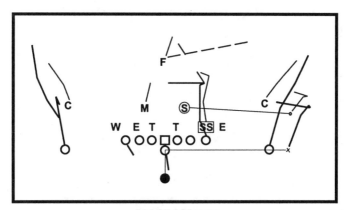

DIAGRAM 5-15
RAM "MOTION CHECK IN" VS. COVER 1
Quarterback chooses the side he wants H to motion to based
on the best match-up possibilities or the wide field. If they
"bump" with motion, he wants to go AWAY from the SS. If they
stay "locked" with motion, he goes TO the SS. His cadence
indicates the direction H will motion—the TE to the call runs
the "Get Open," TE away blocks. H motions to widest position
on called side and runs the "In." Line protects TO the call side.
Good chance to get LB coverage on H.

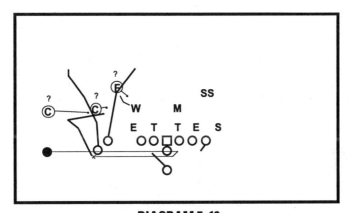

DIAGRAM 5-16
LARRY PAIR X TRACE Y90 X IN VS. BUMPED COVER 1 BLITZ
"Near stack" of bunched receivers created by motion causes
definition problems for bumping, then "re-bumping" defenders.
As X traces back in motion and approaches H & Z, they must
make very fast decisions as to who is #1, #2, and #3. QB peeks
to see if either deep route pops free before throwing the In.

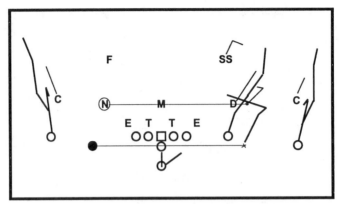

DIAGRAM 5-17
FLEX H8 90 H IN VS. COVER 2 MAN

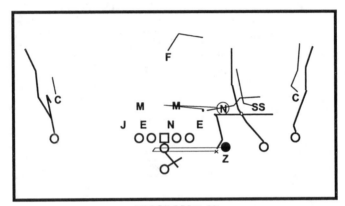

DIAGRAM 5-18
ROY 10 Z TRACE 90 Z OUT VS. COVER 1
Using motion to gain a step and rub defender off for Out. Z,
lined up at #3, is a good match-up vs. Nickel back.

"Banjoed" Man Coverage

The timing and depth with which our In and Out breaks take place cause some unique problems for man defenses that try to switch responsibilities, or "Banjo." Both players originally release in the same direction, and by the time any break is made that crosses the receivers' paths, the hips of both man defenders have probably turned. This hip turn makes the switching process more difficult and takes away the leverage that each defender would normally have in his inside or outside "lane." By the time they have recovered, the ball should have already been delivered to the target successfully.

The other possibility that exists here is that the switch won't be communicated in the right timing, which could result in the defender over the target receiver stopping his feet or breaking on the target receiver. This situation can result in the picker running right by the defender for a big play.

Conceptually, we are again trying to create the best matchups possible for our In and Out against Banjoed man coverage. In this case, though, we may often want our fastest player in the picker spot to give ourselves the best chance at the deep shot.

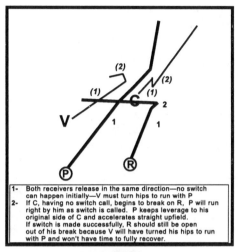

1- Both receivers release in the same direction—no switch can happen initially—V must turn hips to run with P
2- If C, having no switch call, begins to break on R, P will run right by him as switch is called. P keeps leverage to his original side of C and accelerates straight upfield. If switch is made successfully, R should still be open out of his break because V will have turned his hips to run with P and won't have time to fully recover.

DIAGRAM 5-19
IN AND OUT: CAUSING PROBLEMS FOR SWITCHES/BANJOS

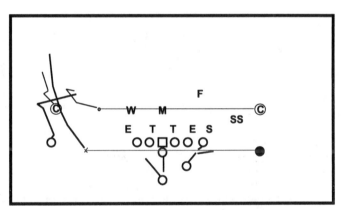

DIAGRAM 5-20
STRONG RIP Z9 MAX 190 X IN VS. BANJOED COVER 1 BLITZ
Two fast players attacking banjoed man coverage.

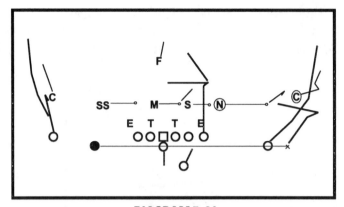

DIAGRAM 5-21
GREEN RIP 11 X10 90 X IN VS. BANJOED COVER 1 FREE
Causing problems for Banjos—N and C must "re-turn" their
hips to execute an assignment switch, and a fast Z could run
right by C if he's not decisive. Motion forces them to make
decisions quickly.

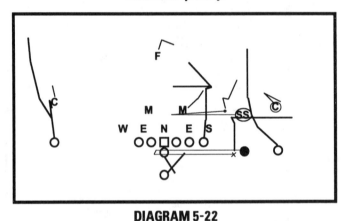

DIAGRAM 5-22
RIP 10 Z TRACE 90 Z OUT VS. BANJOED MAN COVERAGE
C and SS must communicate banjo on the run after motion; C
will have trouble breaking on out because his hips will have
turned inside with #1's pick route by the time a switch is
communicated. If SS stops his feet when #2 starts to break
and then has to switch to the inside route, #1 (a quicker H)
could run right by him.

Zones

As noted before, the best kind of zones against which to run In and Out are those
that aggressively run with routes within their zones and those that play with four
defenders underneath.

Our basic approach to using these routes against zone is to spread those zones out
as much as possible by formation, widening the space between underneath
defenders to open bigger lanes to throw into. Most often, this approach means
using either four- or five-receiver sets. Motion can also be used to create quick

stretches of underneath coverage when the defense may not be totally ready to make a quick, sound adjustment. Ideally, any motion we use would isolate the zone defender off whom we are throwing, separating him from other underneath help.

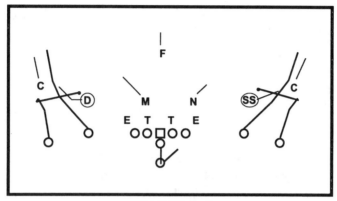

DIAGRAM 5-23
FLEX 90 X AND Z IN VS. COVER 3
Using a wide set to spread a zone defense and widen the lanes between zone drops—QB has symmetrical sides, can pick based on matchup or widest flat defender.

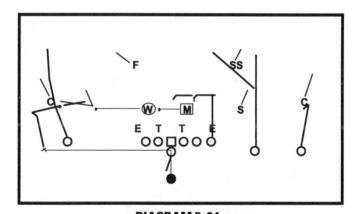

DIAGRAM 5-24
RIP 8 F11 HOT 190 F IN VS. COVER 4
Forcing a fast motion adjustment by defense—F can catch the ball on either side of moving W. Box will be open right in front of QB if M over adjusts.

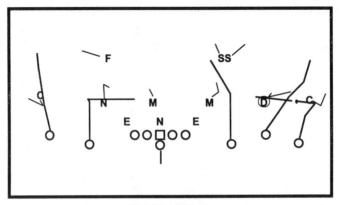

DIAGRAM 5-25
EMPTY HOT 90 Z IN VS. COVER 2
Opening up space between zone defenders with a no-back
set—In can be completed on either side of D, depending on
how he opens his hips.

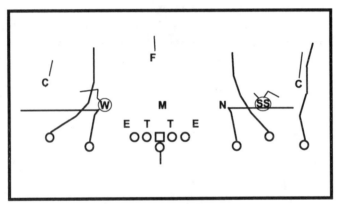

DIAGRAM 5-26
EMPTY HOT 90 F & H OUT VS. COVER 3

The "Swing" Tag

A simple tag that has the ability to help the "In" combination in particular is a basic backfield "Swing." Normally, this type of tag is used against zones in which we want to make sure the flat defender widens so we can get the "In" inside of him. If flat coverage still insists on "hanging" and staying inside, the quarterback will immediately throw the Swing so he can make yardage up the sideline.

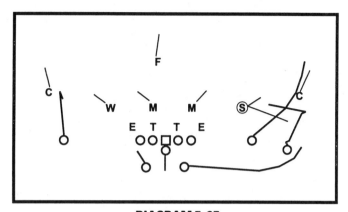

DIAGRAM 5-27
SPLIT REX 190 Z IN H SWING VS. 4-4 COVER 3
Controlling flat coverage who hangs inside #1 with the Swing.

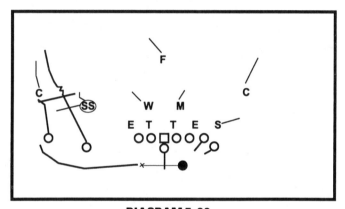

DIAGRAM 5-28
GREEN LARRY PLUS H SHUFFLE STAY 190 X IN SWING VS. COVER 3
SS who wants to hang in "In" lane will give up Swing up the sideline
or widen to Swing and leave "In" open. "Shuffle" motion gets H
started on his wide course without giving LBs much time
to recognize or adjust.

CHAPTER 6

The "Wheel" Route

The "Wheel" route is a simple concept that initially evolved from motion, using three basic routes to take advantage of different ways in which defenses adjust to that movement. Specifically, those three elements are a Slant, a "Wheel," and a Split. The Slant and the Wheel are used to attack flat coverage, taking advantage of the quick, pre-snap stretch that motion can create against zone defenses, while the Split is a built-in "big play" when the motion moves the free safety out of the middle of the field. Our basic route rules are constructed in such a way as to give us optimum flexibility and multiplicity in the way we distribute those routes. However, the sight picture and basic read for the quarterback remain the same.

By building a Slant and potentially a "Stick" route into our backside rules, a full-field horizontal stretch is created that gives us built-in answers even in cases where defensive over rotation to motion eliminates our frontside options.

The Wheel's basic design also lends itself extremely well to the Red Zone; like the Fade and Quick Smash, it is a staple play in this crucial area. It is important for four principle reasons:

1) The Slant routes on either side of the pattern are excellent in terms of their ability to gain separation from different forms of man coverage.
2) The different combinations of formation and motion that we can use with this play can break down a lot of different types of defenses that are played inside the 25-yard line.
3) The Split route gives us a chance at a touchdown strike from the outer edges of the Red Zone.
4) Many times our Red Zone strategy focuses around breaking man coverage while having safe, yard-gaining dump opportunities against zones. While the first three elements help us break man coverage, the route's horizontal stretch enables us to be very sound against zones, especially when defenses rush four or five while playing those zones. Additionally, the Split can break 2 deep coverages for big gains.

Basic 90-190 Wheel Rules

Diagrammed below are three basic forms the Wheel route can take based on the formation, motion, and protection used. It is critical to note, however, that we do not make players memorize three different sets of rules to run the Wheel. Instead, they initially understand their assignments this way:

The motion man will always have the Wheel. The receivers initially lined up at the #1 position on either side will always have Slants. The next receiver inside the frontside Slant who is not blocking will have a Split. Anyone else in the pattern runs a Stick.

That basic formula of assigning routes is illustrated in the three examples that follow.

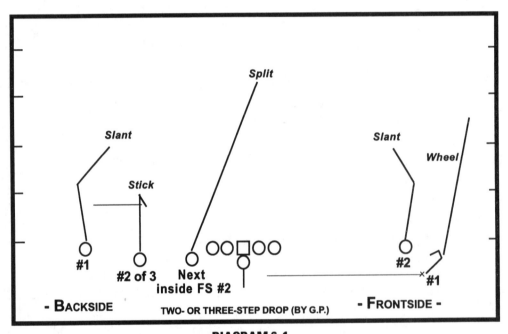

DIAGRAM 6-1
90-190 "WHEEL" PACKAGE BASIC RULES:
WHEEL RECEIVER MOTIONS TO A SINGLE RECEIVER SIDE

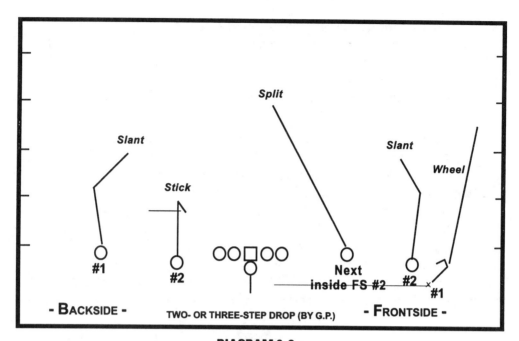

DIAGRAM 6-2
90-190 "WHEEL" PACKAGE BASIC RULES:
WHEEL RECEIVER MOTIONS TO A TWO RECEIVER SIDE

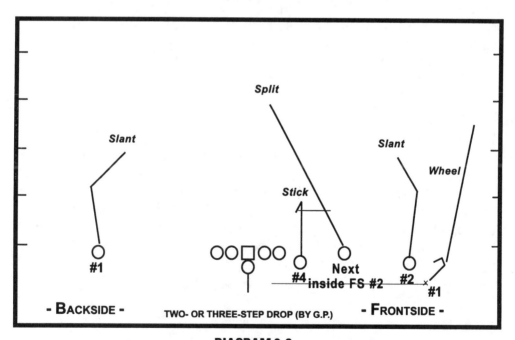

DIAGRAM 6-3
90-190 "WHEEL" PACKAGE BASIC RULES:
WHEEL RECEIVER MOTIONS TO A THREE RECEIVER SIDE

Slant (Frontside). The receiver's basic split is 14 yards plus 2 (two yards wider than the basic Slant split). He should attack the defender over him and break to the Slant at a depth of six yards. The only difference between this Slant and the Slant he runs on 93-193 is that his break must be skinnier than usual because of his relationship with the Wheel and the types of adjustment the motion will create.

Each specific type of coverage demands a specific type of Slant technique, but three things should always be true. First, the receiver's final break must be made distinct, not rounded, by planting off his outside foot, snapping his head and shoulders, and accelerating out of the break. Second, whatever release technique he uses will be for the purpose of gaining inside leverage on the cornerback at some point so he has clean air in which to run, and so the corner does not have a good angle through which to make a play. Third, as the receiver's head snaps inside out of the final break, his hands should come with him as he looks and readies himself for the ball immediately. The timing of the throw may dictate that the quarterback put the ball right on top of him immediately. (See Vol. 1 Chap 7 for specific technique)

Against Cover 2, the receiver must be aware of the outside linebacker on his side; he is the player the receiver must beat, either inside or outside. The receiver should base his angle of break in this case on how he sees the linebacker sliding with the pre-snap motion. If he is relatively stationary and does not come to the receiver too much, there is a good chance the receiver can beat him by staying skinny and outside. If the linebacker bumps over very far at all, the receiver must beat him inside and settle in a central point between his drops and that of the next linebacker inside; the quarterback may be coming to the receiver a bit later than normal.

Wheel: The receiver should work to hug the line of scrimmage on his initial motion, getting up close to the line before turning and moving parallel to the line of scrimmage. He should motion to a point 2 to 3 yards outside the widest receiver on his side, getting a read on the depth of the defender that will end up over him. If the defender that ends up over him is softer than 5 to 6 yards, the receiver simply turns around, faces the quarterback, and looks for the ball. Upon catching it, he snaps his head and shoulders around tightly to the outside and accelerates quickly along the sideline north and south. He should run with a good forward body lean in such a way that he falls forward and gains yardage after contact.

If the defender over him is low, the receiver should convert to a Fade, outside releasing him if at all possible. The receiver's movement should help him, propelling him toward the defender's outside shoulder where he can swim or rip him as he goes by. If the defender over him is a low, Cover 2 corner, the receiver should look for the ball in the Fade hole as soon as he clears him. If the defender plays him, the receiver pins and straightens him, looking for the ball in the space outside him.

Split: The receiver's job is to get to a spot 22 to 25 yards deep over the ball (or over the near guard if he is lined up wider) as quickly as possible, replacing the free safety if he leaves. The receiver is the big play man getting through the trash underneath to find the ball. His technique will vary by coverage, as illustrated below:

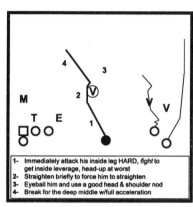

DIAGRAM 6-4
SPLIT TECHNIQUE VS. LOOSE MAN COVERAGE

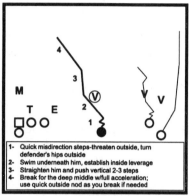

DIAGRAM 6-5
SPLIT TECHNIQUE VS. TIGHT MAN COVERAGE

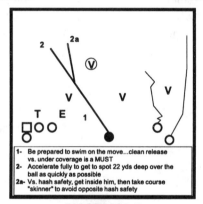

DIAGRAM 6-6
SPLIT TECHNIQUE VS. ZONES

Stick: The receiver releases straight upfield to four yards' depth, plants on his outside foot, and snaps his head inside, just as he would on a Hitch. He should expect the ball immediately. If he does not get the ball quickly, he should work to stay centered between the first and second short defenders inside the cornerback. If he feels pressure from the inside linebacker working outside toward him, he slides back outside parallel to the line of scrimmage, and keeps working that way unless someone crosses his face to the outside. If he gets the ball "late," while sliding, he squeezes the ball and accelerates to the sideline before turning up, just as he would on a normal out-breaking route.

Slant (Backside): The receiver uses a basic Slant split and technique. He should get a feel for where the first short defender inside the cornerback is on his side and get open on either side of him.

Quarterback: The quarterback uses a two- or three-step drop, determined by game plan. Generally, we are more apt to use two-step drops if we think we will be throwing the Wheel short or the Slant quickly; a three-step drop is more likely if we are holding the ball for the Split or a later Slant. The quarterback will know which we are using each practice week.

The quarterback has pre-snap and post-snap jobs on this play. He can not try to do the post-snap jobs before the snap, and he should never attempt to do the pre-snap jobs once the play starts.

The quarterback first pre-snap job relates to finding the free safety and his relationship to motion. If he comes out of the middle, the quarterback knows right away that he will be throwing the Split, wherever the Split is located, once the play begins. The quarterback should never try to throw the split out of rhythm or late. He should throw it based on either a clean pre-snap decision or a distinct Cover 2 read in rhythm (see below).

The other pre-snap job, assuming the Split is not available, is to size up underneath coverage in relationship to the frontside Wheel/Slant combination. If more than one short defender slides into a position to cover the Wheel and Slant, the quarterback knows he is going backside right away, either to a singled Slant beating the backside flat defender, or the Slant/Stick combination off the first short defender.

The quarterback's post-snap job, assuming he is going frontside, is to simply read the flat defender. If he widens to the Wheel, the quarterback hits the Slant inside him, keeping the Slant receiver on a skinny course out of reach of the next short defender. If the flat coverage hangs under the Slant, the quarterback gives the Wheel a shoulder-high ball on his outside number so he can quickly spin and gain yards upfield.

Cover 2 is a special case. Often, if a team stays in Cover 2 even with the motion, they will have more short defenders than the offense can account for frontside, and the quarterback will have gone to the backside via his pre-snap read. If the quarterback did not make this decision, either because of an eight-man drop or for some other reason, he should work the hash safety. If the safety allows the Split inside, the quarterback hits the Split just as he clears. If the safety hangs and the cornerback does not squeeze the Fade hole, the quarterback hits the Wheel man up the sideline. His outlet would be the Slant throttling between defenders, showing his numbers.

The quarterback's reads against different types of coverage, including cases that would cause him to go backside, are depicted in the following diagrams.

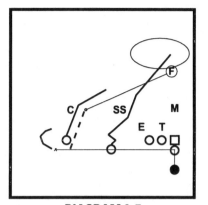

DIAGRAM 6-7
WHEEL READ VS. COVER 1 BLITZ ex. 1:
FS LEAVES TO COVER WHEEL, HIT SPLIT

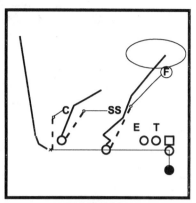

DIAGRAM 6-8
WHEEL READ VS. COVER 1 BLITZ ex. 2:
FS BUMPS OUT OF MIDDLE TO FINAL #3,
SPLIT MUST BEAT HIM, Q.B THROWS TO HIM

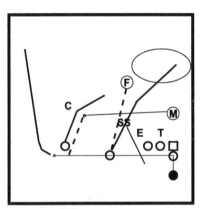

DIAGRAM 6-9
WHEEL READ VS. COVER 1 BLITZ ex. 3:
FS SHOWS BLITZ ALIGNMENT PRE-
SNAP, SPLIT MUST BEAT HIM, Q.B
THROWS TO HIM

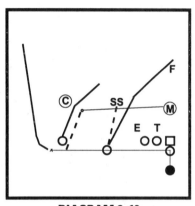

DIAGRAM 6-10
WHEEL READ VS. COVER 1 FREE:
SLANT OR WHEEL, BASED ON MATCHUP
& DOWN/DISTANCE

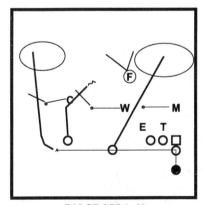

DIAGRAM 6-11
WHEEL READ VS. COVER 2:
SPLIT TO WHEEL OFF F; SLANT INSIDE
OF W IF BOTH TAKEN AWAY

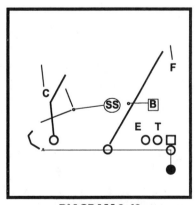

DIAGRAM 6-12
WHEEL READ VS. BASIC COVER 3:
SLANT OR WHEEL OFF SS

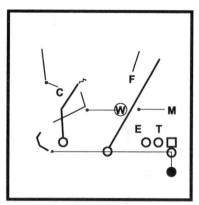

DIAGRAM 6-13
WHEEL READ VS. COVER 4:
SLANT OR WHEEL OFF W

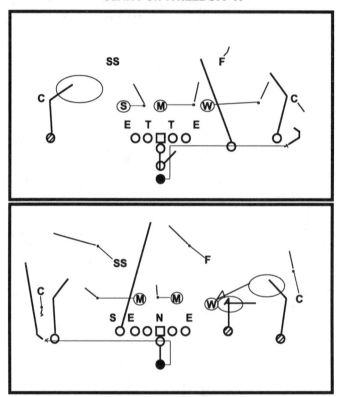

DIAGRAMS 6-14 AND 6-15
EXAMPLES OF PRE-SNAP LB ROTATION THAT CAUSE THE QB
TO WORK BACKSIDE

Using Various Forms of the "Wheel"

As noted before, one of the major strengths of the Wheel route is its ability to take on numerous forms and looks that can provide different types of leverage *without* changing its basic elements or the quarterback's thought process. Illustrations and descriptions of some of these forms follow.

Two-Back Varieties

Motioning from a two-back set to a one-back set to create the Wheel has some distinct advantages over motioning from a one-back look to no-back look. The first of these advantages is that the threat of the run remains, which often limits the distance which multiple linebackers can slide to get into the lanes of the Slant and Wheel routes.

Second, this form of the Wheel keeps normal 90 protection intact, allowing a back to work in the protection from a normal position and eliminating the need to use "hot" protections.

Last, two-back looks for Wheel allow us to line up in sets more basic to the running game before motioning out, which often helps us in our early-down formation sequencing. Three different types of two-back Wheel looks follow.

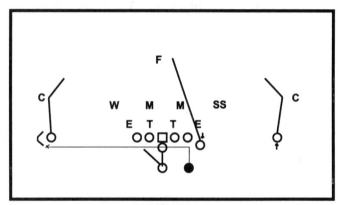

DIAGRAM 6-16
BROWN R H11 190 WHEEL

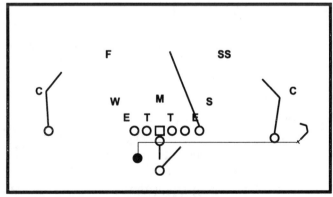

DIAGRAM 6-17
WEAK RIP F10 90 WHEEL

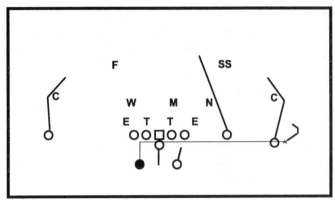

DIAGRAM 6-18
SPLIT REX H10 90 WHEEL

Wheel Away from Trips

Against defenses that over rotate to a trips alignment, motioning away from the three receiver side quickly can create a lot of pressure to the weakside of a defense. In these cases, it is very difficult for a defense to get two short defenders in a position to be a factor in the weakside Slant/Wheel combination. If the free safety works hard to the weakside to help, the Split route coming from the backside becomes a factor.

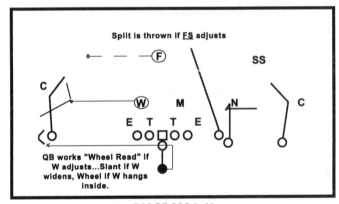

DIAGRAM 6-19
REX OUT F11 HOT 190 WHEEL

Wheel Toward Trips

Motioning the Wheel man toward a pre-existing trips side is very useful because most zone defenses are poorly equipped to handle four receivers to a side, especially in light of the fact that this route requires them to cover a weakside Slant as well. The four receiver threat forces the defense to find a way to get two short defenders in the Slant and Wheel lanes while still having adequate answers for the #3 and #4 receivers.

This type of attack is especially good against coverages and teams that cheat their free safety toward the trips side to help in strongside coverage, rob, or bracket, when the trips is to the wide field *or* free safeties who play in the middle of the field regardless of formation and ball position. Many times, the safety will widen a bit further as an adjustment to the back's motion, which allows the offense to get the Split inside him to the hole in the middle.

Two of the many ways that motion toward trips can be used with the Wheel—one with a sixth protector and one without a sixth protector (which requires "hot" protection)—are illustrated below.

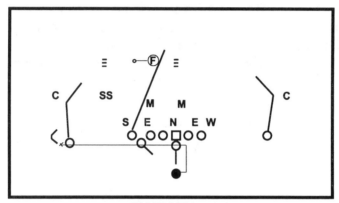

DIAGRAM 6-20
LIZ MINUS H11 F190 WHEEL

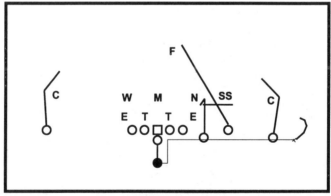

DIAGRAM 6-21
REX 6 F10 HOT 90 WHEEL

Wheel to 2 x 2 Sets

Wheel to a balanced set is an excellent way to get the tight end involved as the man running the Split. At times his involvement is preferable because it is easier for him to get quickly to the middle of the formation, which is the ideal place for the Split to be.

Balanced sets also afford the luxury of having the "Stick" route on the backside to complement the Slant, making the backside option even better if the quarterback feels uneasy about the frontside in any way.

Last, as illustrated in Diagram 6-25, the balance of a 2 x 2 set allows us to use a tool we call "motion check" to maximize our matchups. "Motion check" simply means the quarterback will, in his cadence, indicate which way the remaining back is to go in motion, which will in turn function as a protection check and tell which tight end to block and which to run the Split route. Generally, the quarterback will motion the back to the side of the weakest flat defender.

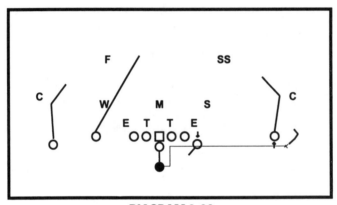

DIAGRAM 6-22
R 11 F10 Y90 WHEEL

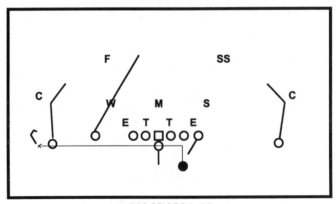

DIAGRAM 6-23
GREEN LARRY 10 F11 Y190 WHEEL

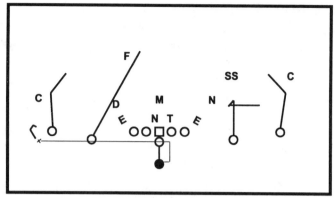

DIAGRAM 6-24
FLEX F11 HOT 190 WHEEL

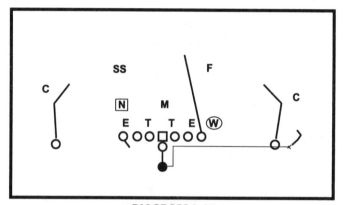

DIAGRAM 6-25
RAM "MOTION CHECK" WHEEL
**QB chooses the side away from best flat defender—in this
case, he sends H in motion away from N. The FB, away from
call, blocks, and Y, to call, runs the Split. Basic read off W
will hold up, with the Split being a possibility if FS widens
too far with motion and SS's rotation doesn't take it away.**

Tags for the Wheel Route

Wheel Trade

"Wheel Trade," which we have also called "Wheel Fade," simply exchanges the jobs
of #1 and #2 frontside. The #1 receiver now runs the Slant and #2 runs the Wheel,
which must convert to the "Fade" portion of the route to stay out of the Slant's
sandbox.

This tag creates an effect very similar to the "In" route (Chapter 5), and is
tremendously effective against multiple types of man coverage. Versus man
coverage that "locks" versus motion, the faster back running the Slant rubs right off
the Fade, creating a real difficulty for the often overmatched linebacker or nickel
player who has run out laterally to cover him. If the man coverage "bumps," a

mismatch is created for the Fade, who will have an easier time than normal establishing outside leverage because of the quick motion. The Split is still excellent against man varieties that make the motion adjustment with the free safety. An example of "Wheel Trade" is shown below.

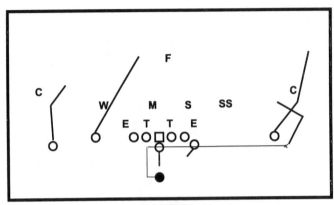

DIAGRAM 6-26
LEX HIP H10 Y90 WHEEL TRADE

Wheel Turn

"Wheel Turn" is a tag solely for the frontside #2 receiver who would normally run a Slant route. In the case of "Wheel Turn," he cuts his split to four yards maximum and runs a basic "Turn" route, just as in the 95-195 package (see Chapter 8). All other elements stay in place exactly as they were for the basic Wheel.

The first two elements of the quarterback's pre-snap progression are still exactly the same: Split if the free safety leaves, go backside if the frontside is overloaded.

The quarterback's frontside read is even simpler, however, for the Wheel Turn than it is for the Wheel: if the man who walks out over the motioning Wheel is "high," or 7 yards off or further, he throws the Wheel quickly; if the man walking out is "low," he hits the Turn, who will beat the next short defender inside and be working out into the open space.

To make this tag work, the motion should get at least 10-12 yards outside the position of the Turn man. The horizontal space created by this motion helps define things for the quarterback, aids the Turn in getting open, and creates a bigger R.A.C. lane for the Turn once he turns upfield.

Illustrations of this basic Wheel Turn read and examples of the multiple ways it can be deployed follow.

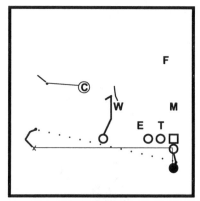

DIAGRAM 6-27
"WHEEL TURN" READ:
HIGH DEFENDER GOES WITH MOTION
Wheel route has no immediate opposition for quick throw; C too soft, flat coverage has too much ground to cover and is walled by the Turn. Pitch & catch for a solid gain.

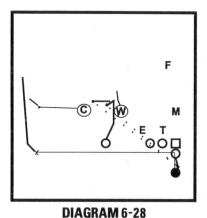

DIAGRAM 6-28
"WHEEL TURN" READ:
LOW *ZONE* DEFENDER GOES
WITH MOTION
Wheel route creates a horizontal stretch, Turn has leverage to the outside on the next defender in.

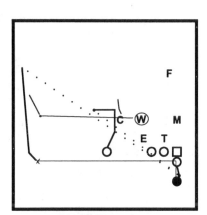

DIAGRAM 6-29
"WHEEL TURN" READ:
LOW *MAN* DEFENDER GOES WITH MOTION
Two viable options: Motioning back may have a speed mismatch on a LB running wide with him on the deep shot; Turn has a good chance, because it will naturally function as a "pressure Out" route being run into a lot of open space.

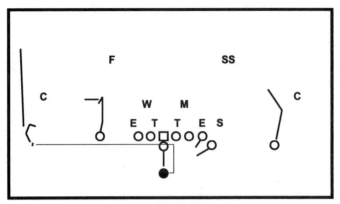

DIAGRAM 6-30
RIP PLUS H11 STAY 190 WHEEL TURN
Using a weakside Wheel Turn combination to create a
possible mismatch for X on the Turn vs. a LB. Tight End/Wing
set to the strongside may lock LBs into a less advantageous
coverage position because of the run threat; also allows a
fuller, double team protection to that side.

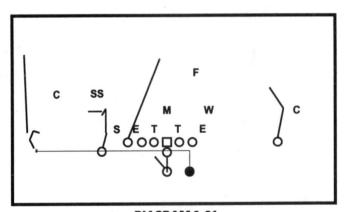

DIAGRAM 6-31
BROWN LIZ H11 190 WHEEL TURN
Wheel Turn to Z on the strong side.

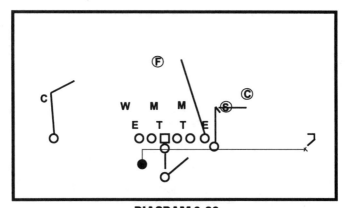

DIAGRAM 6-32
WEAK RIP WING F10 90 WHEEL TURN
Motioning out of a running look to create a quick stretch of
the defense, keeping a back in to avoid the need for "Hot"
protection. Z running the "Turn" can create a good mismatch.

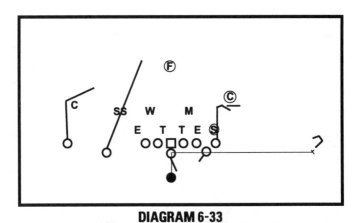

DIAGRAM 6-33
RAY MINUS H10 F90 WHEEL TURN
Stretching the underneath coverage to a Tight End-Wing side

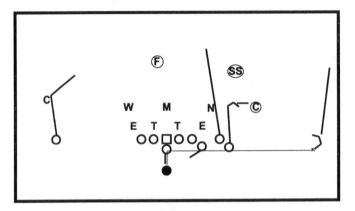

DIAGRAM 6-34
SQUEEZE R 8 F10 Y90 WHEEL TURN
Creating a four-man side and a quick stretch by motioning the
Wheel man wide outside of a bunched set. H becomes #3 to
the called side and runs the Split. If overloaded, as shown to
the squeezed size, QB can always hit the backside Slant.

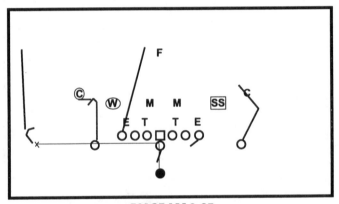

DIAGRAM 6-35
SQUEEZE RAM "MOTION CHECK" WHEEL TURN
QB chooses the side away from best flat defender—in this
case, he sends H in motion away from SS. Y, away from call,
blocks, and FB, to call, runs the Split. X, to the call, runs the
Turn. Ball thrown to X beating M if W leaves with motion, H
on the Wheel if C leaves with motion. If F leaves, of course,
we hit the Split.

CHAPTER 7

Scanning the Horizon: Ideas in Development in the Quick Passing Game

All the routes we have discussed up to this point are things we have had experience applying at different points within our package, and can thus talk with a definite confidence about. In the interest of presenting a genuine product free of "clinic talk," we have distinctly separated those things from the ideas that follow here: ideas that are in the process of theoretical development that may well eventually take their place in our scheme alongside the other quick passes.

We view our offense never as a finished product, but as a constant "evolution" that continues to grow from a sound foundation to ensure we are always giving our personnel the best possible chance to succeed. This evolution comes from a number of different sources, including:

—   Picking up ideas from our contemporaries that we see being used successfully and adapting them to our own structure and the things we do best.
—   Recognizing leverage that we find our offense gaining in certain sets and situations, and designing/creating specific ways to best take advantage of that leverage that we did not have available to us before.
—   Tinkering, experimenting, and brainstorming by our staff that produces good ideas we can make use of.
—   Making adjustments or changes that are needed to cope effectively with trends or developments by defenses that are causing us problems. For example, the advent of Cover 4 and Cover 2 pattern-read principles forced a whole new period of development in our offensive thinking that took us to a "higher level."

The flexibility and comprehensiveness of our system allows us to do this evolving in large part within the framework that already exists so we never have to undertake a major overhaul of our structure to grow and get better. In the example of dealing with pattern-reading, most of the new ideas we have used to successfully attack those defenses have come from tags and adjustments to routes we already have, using concepts that were easy to employ within our existing structure. Not having to reinvent the wheel to have success against a given defense or take advantage of a good idea really helps in terms of the continuity, stability, and teachability of your offense.

It is also very important to us to draw upon all four of those sources of growth as we evolve. While the last of the categories listed may be the most immediately important to having success, it is crucial to be proactive as well as reactive. We want to create new problems for people by being a step ahead of them as or more often than we are reacting to problems they are causing us. The last of those sources listed, vital as it is, is reactive, while the first three are proactive and enable us to stay on that "cutting edge" that forces people to come up with ways to deal with us.

What follows is a peek at our wheels of growth literally as they turn: three routes we are looking at related to our 90-190 series of quick passes, concepts that are pending further development and field testing and could eventually grow into parts of our basic attack.

The "Drive"

The "Drive" route combines elements of the "Short" and the "In" packages, using field width and a potential pick to free up an outside receiver running a Short route. The idea, as with the 97-197, is to read and work off the defender over #2, who runs the "Drive." Enough similarities exist, in fact, that we could easily make "Drive" a *tag* for #2 out of the basic 97-197 package, and simply call "97 Drive" or "197 Drive," without presenting it as an entirely new package. If this defender turns to widen at all, regardless of coverage, the Short will come open into the area he leaves, either off the rub of the Drive (in the case of man coverage), or into the void vacated by the defender we are reading . If the identified defender sits there, either because of his technique within a zone or a "banjo" switching technique within man coverage, the Drive route works off the cornerback, maintaining inside leverage while pressing/chasing him outside to widen the defense. At a certain point, he plants and breaks back inside, a hole having been created by his push and the path of the Short that should turn the second defender to the inside.

It is our opinion that this package has real possibilities against a number of defensive concepts. Against Cover 4, for example, when the outside linebacker over #2 sees a flat-type release, he sprints to cover him since he serves as the flat coverage. This reaction should break the Short wide open into all kinds of running space after the catch.

Likewise, this package gives us a good chance to find the existing holes in the latest defensive trend, the zone blitz, either with the Short or the adjustable Drive. Both of these routes are coming into areas often voided by those schemes, and both have the ability to adjust right into the quarterback's line of vision.

Here's how 90-190 "Drive" would look against the four basic coverages, with the defender we are reading circled.

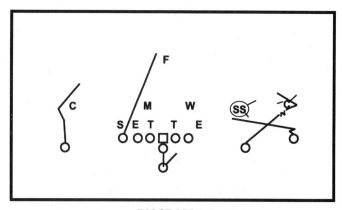

DIAGRAM 7-1
LIZ 8 90 DRIVE VS. COVER 1
SS opens/widens, Short comes open off rub.
If SS hangs in a "Banjo," Drive breaks into open lane, beating
cornerback, who is playing with outside leverage

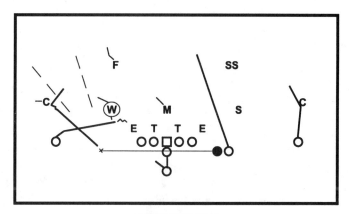

DIAGRAM 7-2
RON PAIR H9 190 DRIVE VS. COVER 2
If W opens outside with #2, Short pops open right inside him;
if he sits on the Short, the Drive has an open lane behind and
outside him after widening the outside leverage corner

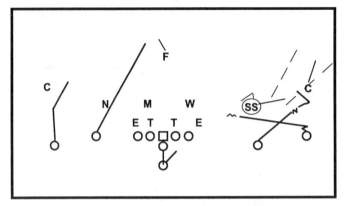

DIAGRAM 7-3
FLEX 90 DRIVE VS. COVER 3
SS opens to flat, Short pops open quickly right inside him;
if SS hangs and squats on Short, Drive breaks inside soft C
into open crease outside and behind SS

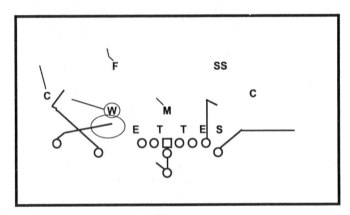

DIAGRAM 7-4
LARRY OUT 190 DRIVE (B TURN) VS. COVER 4
Short broken open when W runs with release to the flat

The "Fin"

The "Fin" is a route possibility that uses three receivers to attack two with crossed releases. The responsibility of the outside receiver is to release under the second, over the top of the third, and hold the short defender over #3 inside. This maneuver isolates the next defender outside, and we choreograph the release and routes of the other two receivers to attack this defender's area in such a way that he can not cover both.

In one sense, this route appears to violate the basic premise that two receivers can not go to the same area, but the timing is such that one receiver arrives just as the other leaves. Because of this timing, the isolated defender is either turning to chase the first, which creates the opening to throw to the second, or not reacting and just settling, which allows us to get the ball to the first.

In our teaching, we would tell the #1 receiver to release inside, find the defender over #3, and attack his upfield hip. If the defender reacts to him and maintains inside leverage, the receiver will sit down close to him and let the defender cover him. If the defender widens toward him as though he may cross his face, the receiver turns his back to him and tries to wall him off. If the defender gets wide of him anyway, the receiver gets in the hole, aware of the next defender inside, and faces the quarterback.

The #2 receiver releases first, over the top of everyone, and angles to the original position of #1, turning up when he gets there. If, as he turns up, he sees the defender we are working off of (the cornerback in any type of Cover 2 or 4 shell, the strong safety in Cover 1 or 3) settle and let him pass, he should turn toward the quarterback in that void he has entered and look for the ball. If the defender reacts and runs with him, the receiver proceeds upfield and makes him chase.

The #3 receiver releases behind the other two, "chasing" the isolated defender in phase with #2. As soon as he sees this defender turn his hips in reaction to #2, he snaps his head inside to get the ball in the void that has been created by this defender's leaving. The only exception to this rule is if he is being chased by man coverage and sees no one else short and outside as the defender leaves. In this case, he would accelerate to the flat and look for the ball. If the isolated defender just sits, the receiver continues to attack him flat to hold him low.

The quarterback looks at the isolated defender off his three step drop. As soon as his hips turn, he is finding the "Fin" being run by #3 as it turns back inside. When he sees him throttling down to turn back inside, the ball is delivered. As the quarterback prepares to throw, he is aware of a possible threat coming from inside to take this throw away, in which case he knows to reset his feet and find #1 as the outlet.

If the defender's hips do not turn and he settles, the quarterback finds a throwing lane and drills the ball into #2 as he clears and turns inside to find the ball.

If man coverage is recognizable, either through motion or pre-snap alignment, the quarterback knows right away that the Fin will come open off two rubs snapping flat to the outside. The fact that the Fin throw is predicated on the non-verbal communication of his intentions by the receiver reduces the error that could come with adjustable reading routes like this one.

Illustrations of the Fin follow.

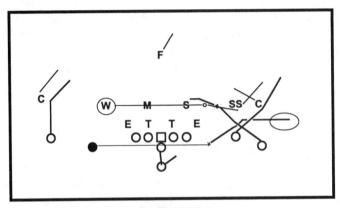

DIAGRAM 7-5
FLEX H6 90 FIN VS. COVER 1
Fin breaks outside off the two rubs

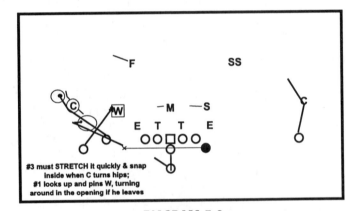

#3 must STRETCH it quickly & snap
inside when C turns hips;
#1 looks up and pins W, turning
around in the opening if he leaves

DIAGRAM 7-6
R 9 Y7 190 FIN VS. COVER 2
**Read the movement of C, coming back inside if W widens
and becomes a factor**

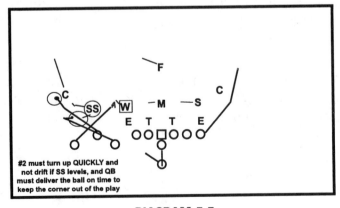

#2 must turn up QUICKLY and
not drift if SS levels, and QB
must deliver the ball on time to
keep the corner out of the play

DIAGRAM 7-7
LARRY 7 190 FIN VS. COVER 3
SS is now the player being read

The "Rub"

The "Rub" is a quick combination between the inside two receivers of a trips set in which we beat the second short defender regardless of his technique and work off the first short defender. It has the lightning-fast tempo of the 95 Turn, and spreads the defense in a similar way. Taught correctly, it appears to have the potential of success against almost any coverage; on a comparison basis, it might be better than Turn against man because of the natural pick, though not quite as good against zone, especially Cover 2.

The #2 receiver, working from outside in, is the man that must read and "beat" the second short defender. Assuming man coverage, he releases at the upfield hip of this man as if to impede him. If the defender is in man, he will be impeded by this course and the ball will be thrown to the out-breaking #3 off this rub right away.

If the defender is in zone, #2 attempts to turn his hips inside, pin him, and spin back out into open space. If this zone defender crosses his face with width and depth, #2 reads it and just sits inside him.

The #3 receiver works to release right underneath the hip of #2 and work this rub, sprinting to the flat area outside at a 2-4 yard depth. He looks for the ball right away.

The #1 receiver runs a clearing Fade with a very wide split, much like #1 in the Turn package. If a Cover 2 cornerback settles and hones in on #3 rather than turning to run, #1 cuts the throttle down to stay open in the hole between corner and safety, turning to the quarterback and looking for the ball.

The quarterback takes a two-step drop and looks for the Shoot by #3 right away, picking up the activity of potential defenders on either side of him. If he's not getting squeezed from anywhere, the ball is delivered on time, right through his hip in stride so he can run in open field after the catch.

If the Shoot is covered effectively by the under defender running from the inside, the quarterback finds #2 adjusting into the opening, either just by sitting or spinning back outside. When eye contact is established, the ball is thrown.

Should the Shoot get heat from outside-in, especially from a cornerback bearing down, the quarterback will have to reset his feet, shuffle, and drill the ball to #1 in the hole behind.

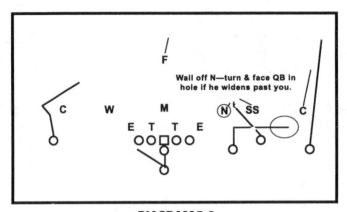

DIAGRAM 7-8
REX 6 90 RUB VS. COVER 1
Rub created for #3 by technique of #2

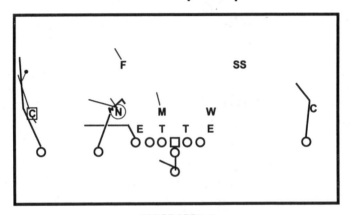

DIAGRAM 7-9
LIZ 9 190 RUB VS. COVER 2
QB reads the reaction of the Nickel player, alert for the
potential of the cornerback collapsing from the outside in.

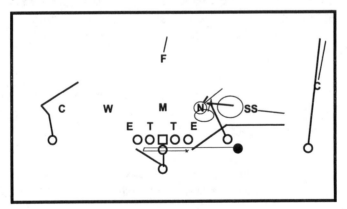

DIAGRAM 7-10
REX OUT H RETURN 90 RUB VS. COVER 3
#2 beats N by sitting if he widens & crosses his face, or
pinning him and whipping back out if he sits. Motion used
to loosen the read player.

The "Hang-Twist"

We, as well as many other teams at the college and professional levels, have begun to make a lot of use of tight end-wing formation concepts because of the running edge they provide, and the coverage problems they can present when set away from two split receivers. As the percentage of time we are in these sets increases, we will need to find ways to make use of them in the passing game as well. One way we may be able to incorporate these sets is with a concept we currently refer to as "Hang Twist."

The basic premise of this route is to take advantage of a defense that does not put two short defenders in a position to cover underneath on the wing side. Using the Fade from the #2 position to clear out, we will then create a two-on-one situation against the outside short defender on the wing side. The Swing has a good chance to gain yards after the catch because of the Fade's clearing out effect, while the "Hang" could be a consistent 6-8 yard catch.

The backfield Swing must get width quickly to stretch this defender. The #1 receiver runs his "Hang," releasing underneath. The #2 receiver works upfield to 5 or 6 yards and turns outside, replacing the short outside defender if he leaves to cover the Swing. The receiver should be aware of the second short defender, beating him by turning outside and continuing to slide outside if he gets inside-out pressure.

The quarterback's only read is the first short defender. The Swing is thrown if he stays or gets bottled up inside, the "Hang" delivered on time if he leaves. Later in the progression, we would teach him to "peek" at the Fade deep in case coverage busted.

As insurance, a "B" tag would likely be used to the opposite side to account for coverages that slid underneath people to the wing side (see Vol. 3 Chap 2). "B Short" would be the prime example of this tag, because having two short defenders to the wing side usually means that only one short defender is left to cover the "Short" combination away from the wing.

A look at how "Hang-Twist" might take shape against different defenses, including an illustration of a situation that might force us away from the "Hang-Twist" side follows.

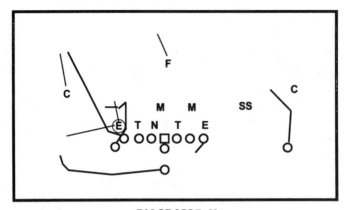

DIAGRAM 7-11
TIGHT RAY OUT X 190 HANG-TWIST VS. COVER 3
Great chance to get the ball to Swinging back in open space
because of M's inside position.

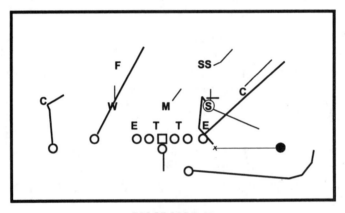

DIAGRAM 7-12
GREEN LARRY 10 H SNUG HOT 90 HANG-TWIST VS. 4-3 COVER 4
S stretched and put in a bind quickly.

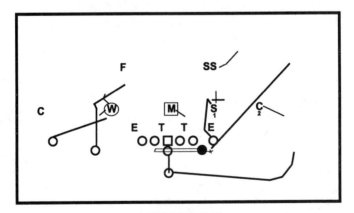

DIAGRAM 7-13
LARRY IN H RETURN HOT 90 HANG-TWIST (B SHORT) VS. COVER 2
Two short defenders to Hang-Twist side; must work Short combination on "B" side. Flaring action by back helps influence M away from
the side we're working.

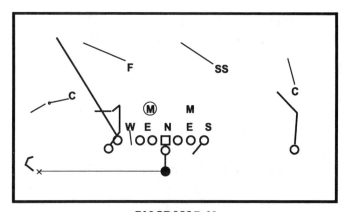

DIAGRAM 7-14
SQUEEZE RIP 9 F LEFT Y 190 HANG-TWIST VS. COVER 3 CLOUD
Motion concept to create a stretch of the zone prior to the snap, X now has the Hang-Twist.

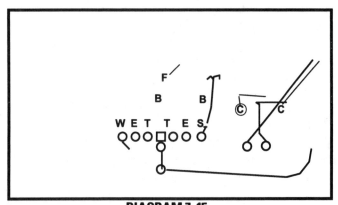

DIAGRAM 7-15
BUNCH RAM X F90 HANG-TWIST (Y OPTION) VS. GOAL LINE COVER 1 WITH "LANES" TECHNIQUE
Hang-Twist attacking at a different width to isolate defender over #2 in a different way. C over #2 plays inside leverage in "Lanes," or "Banjo" technique; release of #1 forces the switch, and his "Hang-Twist" cut breaks back out before inside C can recover. He should get a miniature rub as he "wraps" back under Fade's hip as well. Swing a good outlet.

Tinkering with the "Fade/Out" Combination

Several positive things can happen when we redistribute the routes within our 98-198 "Fade/Out" package, especially within a "Bunched" or "Squeezed" environment. The first benefit occurs against a Cover 2 team that is especially conscious of taking away #1's outside release to the Fade hole and engaging this man over him physically. In this case, by placing the Break Out at the #1 position, we can use him to engage the cornerback, and quickly get the Fade from the #2 position into the deep, outside hole unimpeded. Again, we are taking advantage of the width problem that a squeezed down split can create for a Cover 2 hash safety (see Diagram 8-23).

Second, against man coverages, a sort of "wall" is built for the Fade when it is placed inside the Break Out and possibly the Seam as well. This "wall" makes it difficult for the man covering him to find a clear course through which he can run in covering the Fade, and is especially effective against tight man coverage in the Red Zone. The Break Out times up well for the quarterback to come off to if he sees the Fade has been taken away by deep help.

As with any pass we run from a bunched environment, motion can be used to give us additional leverage and/or confuse the defense. With these routes, we would try to do two things: a) create a "stacked release," and b) confuse coverages that pattern-read or "bump" assignments regarding which player is #1, #2, and #3. By giving the Seam in the latter example the freedom to bend his route into the deep middle, we have, along with the Fade and Break Out, built-in ways to capitalize on different types of defensive breakdowns in this regard.

Systematically, the words we use to get into these concepts are "Trade" and "Outside." "Trade" tells the #1 and #2 receivers in any route to exchange jobs (for another example, see the Trade tag for the "Turn" route in Chapter 4), which, in a two-receiver rule, moves the Break Out to #1 and the Fade inside to #2.

"Outside" moves the routes of #2 and #3 "outside" to the #1 and #2 positions. "Outside 98" from a trips set moves the Seam route normally run by #2 to the #1 position, while the Break Out normally residing at #3 is now run by #2. When using the Outside tag, we have to tell #3 specifically what to do. A full call, then, might be "Outside 98 H Fade," H being the #3 receiver.

Illustrations of these "redistributed" Fade concepts follow.

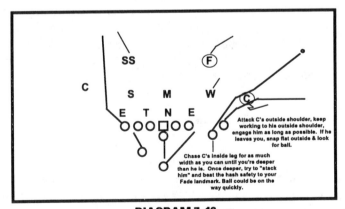

DIAGRAM 7-16
SQUEEZE STRONG RAY 98 TRADE VS. COVER 2
Break Out absorbs and stretches the jam of C, providing a free corridor for #2 to get to the Fade hole.

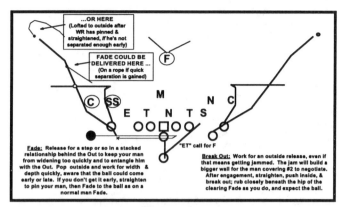

DIAGRAM 7-17
TWIN X RETURN 198 DOUBLE TRADE VS. MAN COVERAGE
Creating a "wall" vs. man coverage while trying to give the defense definition problems through motion. The quarterback works to the side away from FS movement.

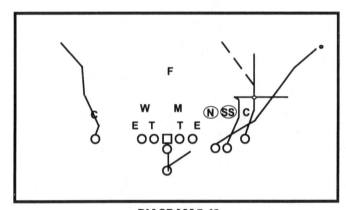

DIAGRAM 7-18
SQUEEZE REX 6 OUTSIDE 98 H FADE VS. BANJOED COVER 1
Two players now create an impediment for the man attempting to cover the Fade from the inside. Banjo technique is rendered ineffective because all three receivers take an outside release initially, no defensive leverage or switching can occur.

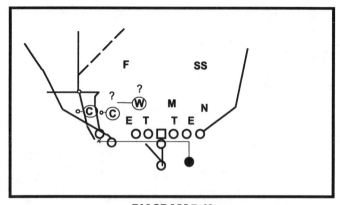

DIAGRAM 7-19
SQUEEZE BROWN LARRY H11 OUTSIDE 198 Z FADE VS.
COVER 2 MAN WITH A "BUMPED" MOTION ADJUSTMENT
Creating identification/definition problems for bumping man
defenders; two deep receivers on deep hash safety.

"Split Alert" with Backfield Motion

This concept would extend part of the basic "Wheel" principle that says we want to strike deep down the middle quickly if the free safety leaves with backfield motion. We can simply add a tag such as "alert," telling a specific receiver on any given route that we want him to run a "Split" route, replacing the free safety if he runs with backfield motion. If the free safety does not run, nothing changes for this receiver, who will usually be the inside most player away from the motion. This tag would allow a team to always take advantage of this big play possibility rather than try to guess the right time to call the "Wheel" route. The only additional read is pre-snap, which means nothing has been complicated for anyone: if the free safety leaves, the quarterback is always going to throw the Split; if the free safety stays, the quarterback executes his normal read.

Examples of how this tag might be used are depicted in the following illustrations.

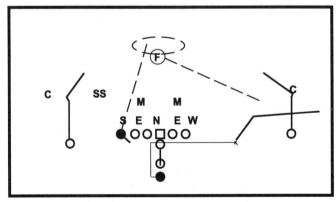

DIAGRAM 7-20
LIZ H8 93 "Y ALERT"

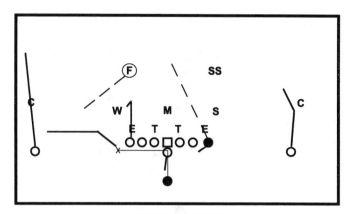

DIAGRAM 7-21
RAM H7 195 "Y ALERT"

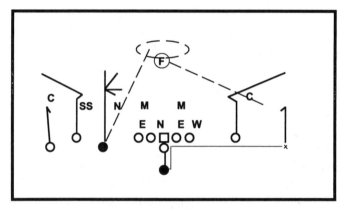

DIAGRAM 7-22
LEX 7 F10 HOT 196 "H ALERT"

Stacked Release Concepts

The concept of releasing receivers in such a way that they appear to the defense to be "stacked" one on top of another could very easily and effectively be applied to two of our basic quick routes.

The stacked release idea is not unfamiliar to people who have employed "Squeeze" and "Bunch" looks in their offense, but we are discovering through our own development and conversations with other coaches, particularly at places like the University of Oregon and Harbor College, that the same principles can be used out wide.

Stacked releases would appear to have their greatest effect on man coverage because they create confusion and momentary indecision that make the break on the final cut much more difficult. Traditionally, man-to-man defense has depended on a certain "locking in" on the part of the defender that allows him to maintain a tight relationship on his receiver. With two receivers running one behind another, not only can those defenders not establish that vital relationship, they in many cases (especially banjo techniques) are not sure who their man is until the final break. This confusion could also cause severe problems for pattern-read defenses because their definitions for walling and release reading are based on #1, #2, #3, and so forth. Stacked releases prevent them from being able to define relative positions in that way since the receivers are lined up one behind another.

To create this mechanism, we would simply add the word "Stack" in front of a basic route package call. The word "Stack" would tell the receivers to stem their routes in such a way that they got into a relationship where one was directly behind another before they pushed upfield. The idea is for them to break as close to the same time as possible.

Obviously, "Stack" has implications for receiver splits, as they must line up relatively close to be able to achieve this relationship in the proper timing. Short motion is also a good tool to get them stacked quickly. The quarterback's timing is affected as well, because he will have to hold the ball a bit longer than he normally would on his three step drop. On occasion, we might even change his drop to a very quick five steps.

The two routes to which this device best applies are the 96-196 "Quick Smash" and the 98-198 "Fade/Out" route packages. In the case of the former, we would release the Smash route behind the Hitch and look for him first, giving the Hitch the ability to maneuver a bit once he broke in front of the Quick Smash. The maneuverability would allow the quarterback to come off to him as a second look.

The stacked Fade/Out would primarily be used as a ball-possession tool to help the Break Out, releasing behind the Fade. The quarterback would look to deliver this pass on time right out of the break to minimize defensive recovery time, unless both defenders completely busted and gave us the Fade for free.

Different ways in which we might employ this "Stack" call are illustrated below.

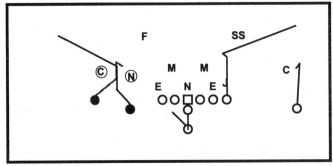

DIAGRAM 7-23
RIP 9 "STACK" 196

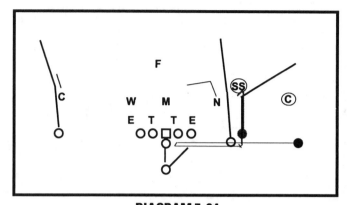

DIAGRAM 7-24
REX IN Z RETURN "STACK" 96

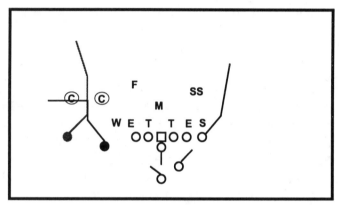

DIAGRAM 7-25
STRONG LARRY "STACK" 198

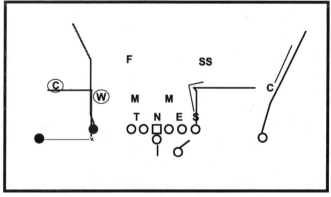

DIAGRAM 7-26
GREEN LARRY 10 X SNUG "STACK" 198

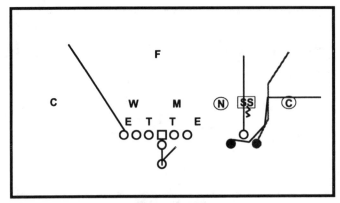

DIAGRAM 7-27
BUNCH RAY 6 "STACK" 98
Great answer against any coverage or defense that tries
to jam #2 hard...Break Out releases right under it, his man
is left with a big traffic jam to negotioate, and the cornerback is isolated 2 on 1.

Modifying the Basic "Seam Read": Turn Tag for #2

For quarterbacks who have difficulty driving the Seam route into the hole that opens when flat coverage widens quickly to an outside route, giving a split #2 receiver a "Turn" route would pose a viable, ball-control alternative that changes very little for the quarterback's thought process and creates a higher percentage throw. If flat coverage *does* widen, the Turn route by #2 simply turns outside into the area the flat defender vacated. The quarterback is reading the same thing that he would in a normal Seam read, except that he knows to throw the Turn rather than the Seam when flat coverage widens. If the flat coverage *does not* widen, he throws the outside route as he normally would.

Because we do not want an inside break by an outside receiver turning in toward an outside break by an inside receiver, this tag would not apply to 91/191 Hitch. The other Seam read routes—92/192 Quick Out and 94/194 Stop—with the outside man breaking outside can make great use of the Turn by #2, especially on a medium distance possession down. Another benefit the Turn tag provides for these routes is that it effectively addresses the "Cover 4 problem" that occurs for the Seam read versus 4-deep type defenses because the hash safety is taken out of the picture (see Vol. 1 Chap 8 for a full description of this "Cover 4 problem").

Illustrations of the Turn tag in both route packages follow.

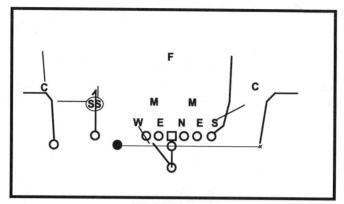

DIAGRAM 7-28
LARRY 7 H6 192 TURN VS. COVER 3
SS the read player—QB hits Turn route replacing him if SS widens
to Quick Out. Formation used to increase the likelihood that S, not
W, will be the drop OLB, putting M in a tough position to get to Turn.

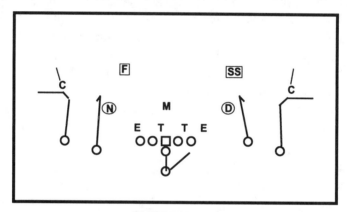

DIAGRAM 7-29
FLEX 92 DOUBLE TURN VS. COVER 4
Turn takes hash safeties out of the play, isolating N and D on 2 short
routes. M too far away to provide substantial help because of wide set.

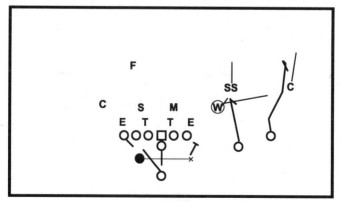

DIAGRAM 7-30
STRONG RAY F SHUFFLE MAX 94 TURN VS. QUARTERS
W controlled by Turn route.

Four-Step Drops

Another idea in development which we would use to help the timing and rhythm of certain three- and five-step passes is a "four-step" drop by the quarterback. Depending on the skills and mannerisms of the players we have at both receiver and quarterback, certain routes from our "quick" package leave the quarterback waiting longer than we would like if he executes even a "three steps and hold" drop. In some years, routes like the "Stop," the "Whip" variation of the Quick Smash, and the "Plant" tag off the "Short route fall distinctly into this category. Conversely, certain routes from our five-step attack materialize too quickly for the quarterback to get the ball where it needs to go on time if he drops five steps. The idea behind the unorthodox four-step drop, then, would be to achieve an "in between" type of timing to accommodate both of these types of routes.

We have played with two different forms of the four-step drop. Each form is an "extension" of other, more basic drops, so a lot of the teaching elements are the same. The first, a variation of the "3 quick" drop, would be to "back out" the first two steps, gaining as much depth as possible by reaching with the foot to the throwing side, reaching again in the two-step backpedal with the off foot, then turning the shoulders perpendicular to the line of scrimmage on the last two steps, which are "hippity hop" steps just as on the "3 quick" drop. If the "3 quick" drop is summarized by saying "*first step reach, hippity hop*," this form of the four-step drop could be summarized with the phrase "*back out/reach 1,2, hippity hop.*" This drop is illustrated below.

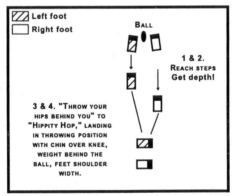

DIAGRAM 7-31
FOUR STEP DROP (Version 1)
FOR A RIGHT HANDED PASSER

The alternate form would simply be an extension of the 2-step drop. Again, the first two steps are "backpedal" steps to gain depth. In this case, however, the quarterback steps with the foot opposite his throwing arm so that, after the second step, he is in position to execute normal two-step drop footwork. This drop becomes, then, essentially a normal two-step drop that has had two backpedal "depth" steps added onto the front of it. This version of the four-step drop, both left and right, is illustrated below.

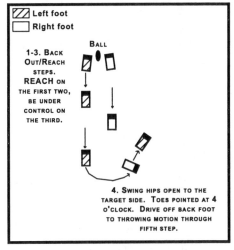

DIAGRAM 7-32	DIAGRAM 7-33
FOUR-STEP DROP (Version 2)	FOUR-STEP DROP (Version 2)
TO THE RIGHT	TO THE LEFT
(RIGHT HANDED PASSER)	(RIGHT HANDED PASSER)

Other In-Breaking Concepts: The "Speed In" and the "Frame"

The "Speed In" and "Frame" are two additional quick route combinations to which we have been exposed but have not actually put into practice as of this writing. Both represent ways to incorporate the advantages of in-breaking routes into quicker, three-step drop actions.

The Speed In

Introduced to us originally by Ron Jenkins, the offensive coordinator at Los Angeles Harbor College, the "Speed In" is generally a single receiver route that can be an effective complement to the Hitch and the Quick Out when a coverage's flat defender works to a wide spot very quickly.

The Speed In break is the exact opposite of the Quick Out; the receiver pushes vertically to four yards' depth, rolls as though "running around a corner," and flattens at six yards, looking to get into the "window" inside the first short defender.

In addition to being good against zones with wide flat defenders, the Speed In has good possibilities against man coverage because it is a flatter break than the normal angled break of a Slant that cornerbacks are more accustomed to defending. The "speed turn" also gives the receiver a good chance to maintain acceleration *through the break*, which is vital against man coverage.

Shown below are two examples of packaged Speed In combinations: first, a basic version, and the second with a "Swing" from the backfield to help widen the flat defender.

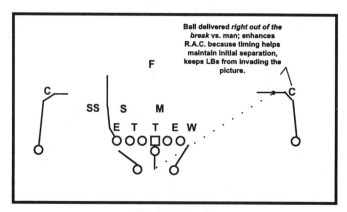

DIAGRAM 7-34
SPLIT LIZ 90 SPEED IN VS. COVER 1

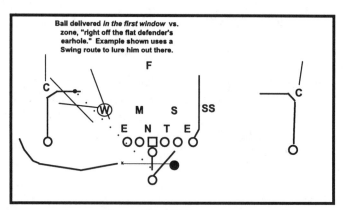

DIAGRAM 7-35
STRONG RIP F SHUFFLE 190 SPEED IN F SWING VS. COVER 3

The Frame

The "Frame" is a trips concept that we were introduced to in a clinic presentation by Jim Donnan, now at the University of Georgia. It is so named because the quarterback's read essentially consists of looking through a "frame" to the #2 receiver as he breaks in and deciding whether the frame is open, is being "invaded" from the inside out, or is being "invaded" from the outside in.

Both the #1 and #2 receivers use Speed In techniques, though at different depths to time the development of the read up in the correct manner. The break of the #1 receiver starts at 6 and rolls to 8, while the break of #2 starts at 4 and rolls to 5 or 6. The #3 receiver outside releases and runs a Seam.

As noted, the QB's read is to look through a "Frame" into the throwing lane surrounding #2's final break. If it is open, he will hit #2 out of his cut on time. If the frame is collapsed on from the outside in (for example, by a SS who has flat responsibility, but "sits" on him, having not yet seen a flat threat from #1), he hits #1 breaking into the lane behind. Should the frame be invaded from inside out, the Seam is delievered on rhythm, being aware of the next danger linebacker in front.

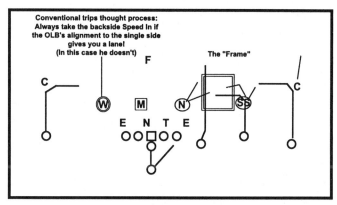

DIAGRAM 7-36
REX 6 90 FRAME VS. COVER 3

The simplicity of this teaching holds up against any coverage. For example, against any kind of man coverage, the Frame will automatically be invaded from outside in, and the ball will go to the outside man breaking into an open lane. This dynamic is illustrated below.

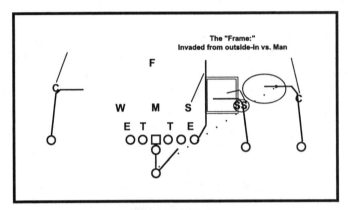

DIAGRAM 7-37
RIP 8 90 FRAME VS. COVER 1 FREE

Andrew Coverdale spent the past football season as the Quarterbacks and Tight Ends Coach at Taylor University. Prior to working at Taylor, he coached for three years at the high school level. While at Northwestern High School in Kokomo, Indiana, he was promoted to Offensive Coordinator and gave clinic presentations on the Tigers' "Bunch" Passing Package. At Noblesville High School, he coached receivers, during which time a player under his direction broke the school record for receptions and earned AAAAA all-state honors.

Coverdale has previously coauthored, *The Bunch Attack*. He has contributed in articles in both the Indians and Wisconsin quarterly coaches' manuals, and works as a receiver's instructor at the Bishop-Dullaghan Passing Clinic. He may be contacted via e-mail at: andy_coverdale@mail.nobl.k12.in.us or aecover@sprynet.com

Dan Robinson spent the past two seasons as the Offensive Coordinator at Taylor University, after being a high school head coach for 13 years at Northwestern High School. Prior to his duties at Northwestern, he was the Offensive Coordinator at East Central High School for nine years.

During his tenure at Northwestern, the Tigers became known for their pro passing attack and explosive offense, which helped produce two undefeated regular seasons, four Mid-Indiana Conference titles, and a trip to the Indiana AAA State Championship Game. The Tigers were among the state's top ten passing teams several times during his tenure, leading the state in 1983. Six quarterbacks under Coach Robinson's tutelage earned all-state honors.

He has worked various summer camps for many years, including the Bishop-Dullaghan Passing Clinic, where he wrote the camp's receiver manual. He has also lectured at clinics throughout Indiana and the Midwest on different aspects of Northwestern and Taylor's offense, and published several articles on different aspects of offensive football. Robinson has also coauthored *The Bunch Attack* with Coach Coverdale. He may be contacted via e-mail at: robinsond@nwsc.k12.in.us

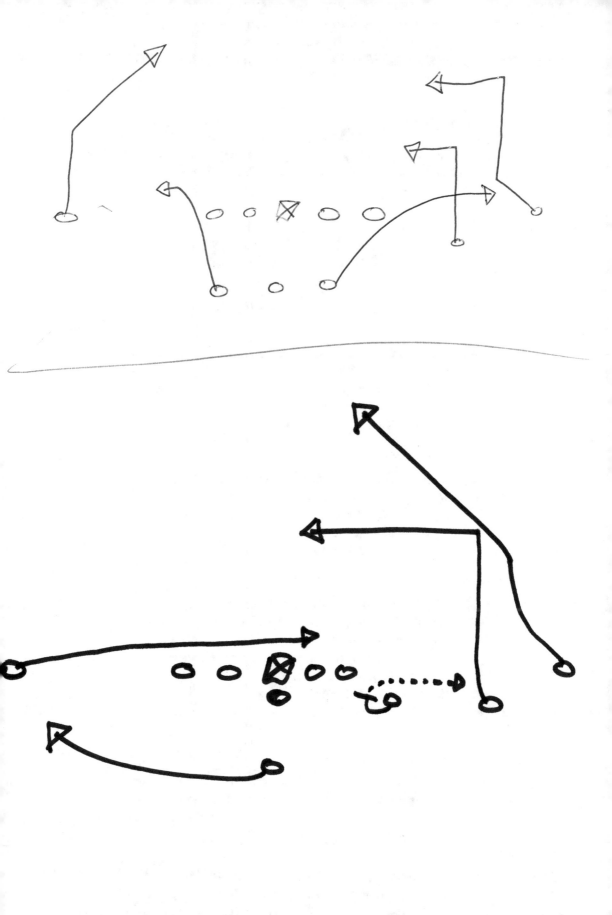

ADDITIONAL FOOTBALL RESOURCES FROM

COACHES ≡ CHOICE

■ *FOOTBALL'S QUICK PASSING GAME*
VOL 1: FUNDAMENTALS AND TECHNIQUES
by Dan Robinson and Andrew Coverdale
1998 ▪Paper▪ 164 pp
ISBN 1-57167-155-2 ▪ $17.95

■ *FOOTBALL'S QUICK PASSING GAME*
VOL 3: IMPLEMENTING THE PACKAGE
by Dan Robinson and Andrew Coverdale
1998 ▪Paper▪ 264 pp
ISBN 1-57167-192-7 ▪ $19.95

■ *THE BUNCH ATTACK*
USING COMPRESSED FORMATIONS IN THE
PASSING GAME
by Dan Robinson and Andrew Coverdale
1997 ▪Paper▪ 260 pp
ISBN 1-57167-044-0 ▪ $19.00

TO PLACE YOUR ORDER:
U.S. customers call
TOLL FREE (800)327-5557,
or write
COACHES CHOICE Books, P.O. Box 647, Champaign, IL 61824-0647,
or FAX: (217) 359-5975